D0429614

Winnie-the-Pooh
on Success

Winnie-the-Pooh

on Success

*In which You, Pooh
and friends learn about
the Most Important
Subject of All*

Roger E. Allen
and
Stephen D. Allen

A DUTTON BOOK

DUTTON
Published by the Penguin Group
Penguin Putnam Inc., 375 Hudson Street, New York, New York 10014, U.S.A.
Penguin Books Ltd, 27 Wrights Lane, London W8 5TZ, England
Penguin Books Australia Ltd, Ringwood, Victoria, Australia
Penguin Books Canada Ltd, 10 Alcorn Avenue, Toronto, Ontario, Canada M4V 3B2
Penguin Books (N.Z.) Ltd, 182–190 Wairau Road, Auckland 10, New Zealand

Penguin Books Ltd, Registered Offices:
Harmondsworth, Middlesex, England

First published by Dutton, an imprint of Dutton Signet,
a member of Penguin Putnam Inc.

First Printing, November, 1997
10 9 8 7 6 5 4 3 2

Copyright © Roger E Allen and Stephen D. Allen, 1997

Grateful acknowledgment is made to the Trustees of the Pooh Properties for the use of
illustrations by E. H. Shepard and quoted material by A. A. Milne.

Individual copyrights for text quotations and illustrations: *Winnie-the-Pooh*, copyright 1926
by E. P. Dutton & Co., Inc.; copyright renewal 1954 by A. A. Milne. *The House At Pooh
Corner*, copyright 1928 by E. P. Dutton & Co., Inc.; copyright renewal 1956 by A. A.
Milne.
All rights reserved

 REGISTERED TRADEMARK—MARCA REGISTRADA

Library of Congress Cataloging-in-Publication Data is available.

Printed in the United States of America
Set in Goudy

Without limiting the rights under copyright reserved above, no part of this publication
may be reproduced, stored in or introduced into a retrieval system, or transmitted,
in any form, or by any means (electronic, mechanical, photocopying, recording, or
otherwise), without the prior written permission of both the copyright owner
and the above publisher of this book.

This book is printed on acid-free paper. ∞

To Marilyn and Stasia.
And to Colter Blake Allen, newest addition to
the Allen family

Acknowledgments

We'd like to thank the excellent staff of the Tacoma Public Library, especially Patricia Vance and Meg Justus, researchers who find answers to the difficult questions, and David Domkoski, who brings authors and the community together.

CONTENTS

Introduction

A long, long time ago—when Winnie-the-Pooh was a very, very young bear and Christopher Robin would still answer "Go to the Zoo" anytime someone asked, "What would be your very favorite thing in all the world to do today?"—almost everyone agreed on what "Success" was.

If we look at a dictionary of that time we find "Success" defined as "the attainment of wealth, position, honors, or the like." That was it. Period! And that had been it in Western society for hundreds of years and maybe even longer. Even when that wasn't what you wanted the culture pushed you in that direction.

Christopher Robin, saying good-bye to Pooh in that enchanted place on the top of the Forest, felt that, as he grew up, he would no longer be able to do what *he* liked best. What he called "Doing Nothing."

"How do you do Nothing?" asked Pooh, after he had wondered for a long time.

"Well, it's when people call out at you just as you're going off to do it, What are you going to do, Christopher Robin, and you say, Oh, nothing, and then you go and do it."

"Oh, I see," said Pooh. . . .

Then, suddenly again, Christopher Robin, who was still looking at the world, with his chin in his hands, called out "Pooh!"

"Yes," said Pooh.

"When I'm—when—Pooh!"

"Yes, Christopher Robin?"

"I'm not going to do Nothing any more."

"Never again?"

"Well, not so much. They don't let you."

Sometime around the middle of this century or thereabouts, the traditional definition of Success held and espoused by "They" began to be challenged. In 1948 Thomas Merton, in his book *The Seven Story Mountain*, wrote, "Success—the logic of worldly success rests on a fallacy: the strange error that our perfection depends on the thought and opinions and applause of other men."

Now as we approach the beginning of a new millennium, more and more individuals are agreeing with Thomas Merton. They are deciding for themselves what Success is, and it may, or may not, include achieving wealth, position, honors, or the like. Individuals are actively exploring new ways to structure their lives and careers. Many are helping to shape a resurgence of spirituality and developing an appropriate philosophy of virtues and moral values. Still others are transforming relationships and social structures and investing in personal growth using old and new tools, techniques, and knowledge. What is more, having decided what Success means to themselves, they are consciously taking the risk and working to achieve it.

This new approach to Being Successful might well be expressed by a Chinese proverb: "There are many paths to the top of the mountain, but the view is always the same."

What isn't the same is that the path taken to reach the summit may no longer be well marked, paved, broad, and straight. It is usually easier to follow the well-traveled road than it is to plan, hack, and carve your own path to the heights.

Which is why we decided to write this book. Obviously, we can't promise that reading *Winnie-the-Pooh on Success* will make you a Success (however you define it). But we do believe that the tried and tested tools, techniques, principles, and procedures that we have included here will make *your* chosen path to the summit of *your* success easier and faster to travel. Their use has helped our clients and ourselves achieve what was wanted. We believe it can do the same for you, and we think you will enjoy the journey and the view.

At this point Eeyore wandered over from the window box where he had been tasting and testing a new species of thistle that he had asked us to plant for him and asked us what we were writing.

We explained that it was the beginning of our new book on Success and about how it would help individuals to define and achieve their own version of success.

Eeyore thoughtfully chewed the last of the thistle and then he nodded.

"I can understand why many would want to do that sort of thing," he said slowly. "After all, only a few of us are fortunate enough to be *Equus asinus*. That's a donkey, you know."

Eeyore considerately paused to be sure that we understood. "Sad But True," he said gloomily, looking back at the window box to see if there were any thistles he had missed while he was talking to us.

"Actually," Eeyore continued, "I'm thinking about a new career myself—personal growth and whatnot, and et ceteras, you know. I'm considering becoming an economist. Actually, I didn't think of that myself. Owl suggested that I might be suited for it. He said someone called Thomas Carlyle said economics was the Dismal Science. That sounds most interesting."

Before we could say anything, Eeyore murmured something about having to go and see about a new thistle field and moved off, so we went back to our writing.

Before we begin, there are two things we should explain. However, if you've read either *Winnie-the-Pooh on Management* or *Winnie-the-Pooh on Problem Solving* you can skip the rest of this introduction (unless you want to refresh your memory) and get a head start on those who haven't.

The first thing is that the adventures of Winnie-the-Pooh and friends (who very nicely again gave us permission) are used, because in our consulting work we have found that people learn more and remember better if we use their adventures to illustrate what is to be learned. Psychologists call this technique "Placing Material to Be Learned in an Unfamiliar Context." As Pooh commented, "Like in the Hundred Acre Wood."

The second thing is that in *Winnie-the-Pooh on Management*, Pooh met The Stranger in the Hundred Acre Wood near the Bee Tree. The Stranger asked Pooh's help in writing a book on management basics. The Stranger is called that because that is the name Pooh thought of at the time, though perhaps he really didn't and we just thought he did, and it stuck, even though it isn't a real name.

As Winnie-the-Pooh, whose real name is Edward Bear, would say, "Some have nicknames and some haven't, and There It Is."

That's all you really need to know to begin. So come with us to the Hundred Acre Wood where some wonderful friends wait to learn with us.

I

In which Owl Finds The Stranger, the Success Formula Is Introduced, and Eeyore Becomes a Poohstick

No one ever knew how it was that Owl found The Stranger. One moment Pooh, Piglet, Eeyore, Owl, and Roo were all sitting around the Bee Tree and talking, and Pooh was getting more and more confuzzled, and the next moment Owl had taken off and flown into the distance.

Several days later, when Owl returned, The Stranger was with him.

"Hallo, Pooh!" cried The Stranger, when he was still some way off. "Hallo, Piglet! Hallo, Eeyore!"

Pooh, Piglet, Eeyore, and Roo were gathered at the bridge and had just finished a long round of Poohsticks. Owl flew up and perched on one of the posts of the bridge and The Stranger climbed up and sat on one of the railings, which bent ominously, as though it might not be able to support him for very long.

"Best be careful," said Eeyore. "Or else you'll wind up a Poohstick." And he shivered, remembering what it was like to *be* a Poohstick.

"I came as quickly as I could," said The Stranger. "Owl said that you had a problem that only I could help with."

"Oh, yes. Well, it's just this," said Pooh. "We were saying how nice it was that I learned how to be a Very Important Bear (VIB) by mastering the fundamentals of Management, and that I have been most fortunate to become a Problem-Solving Bear (PSB), but that I think there's something missing. . . ." And here Pooh stopped talking and with one paw to his head and the other tucked across underneath his arm he looked up and tried to think.

A very faint cracking sound came from where The Stranger was sitting, but the only thing that happened was that Eeyore rolled his eyes and Pooh continued to think. After a long while of Pooh thinking, Piglet hopping up and down nervously, Eeyore waiting for The Stranger to become a Poohstick, and The Stranger patiently waiting, Pooh continued.

"I think," he started, "that I want to *do* something."

"What?" asked The Stranger.

"That's the part that has me confuzzled," said Pooh. "I want to use what I've learned. I want to . . . I want to be . . ."

"Successful?" asked The Stranger.

"Yes," said Pooh. "Success Full!"

"Me too! Me too!" cried Piglet and Roo.

"You already are successful," said The Stranger. "In many ways."

"Am I?" said Pooh. "I mean, I want to use what I've learned to *do* something. Something Important. Something that will be a Success."

"I have something that I think will help," said The Stranger. "It is called the Success Formula."

Pooh wrinkled his nose and made a face. "What does it taste like?" he asked.

"It's not *that* kind of formula, Silly Bear," said The Stranger, restraining a chuckle. "It is like the SOLVE problem-solving method. It is a way of systematically defining what it is you want to do, and then helping you to do it."

"Like SOLVE helped to solve problems!" said Piglet.

"Exactly," said The Stranger. And he took a sheet of paper out of his case and began writing on it. When he was finished, he turned it around and showed it to his friends. This was what he had written:

Select a Dream

Use Your Dream to Set a Goal

Create a Plan

Consider Resources

Enhance Skills and Abilities

Spend Time Wisely

Start! Get Organized and Go

"It spells 'Suchness'!" shouted Piglet, who looked at everything The Stranger wrote now to see what it spelled, because it usually spelled something, and Piglet liked being the one who noticed first.

"Close, Piglet," said The Stranger. "It spells 'Success.' "

"That's what I meant," said Piglet.

"And it is one of those acro- whatevers," said Pooh.

"Yes," said The Stranger. "It is another acronym. It is intended to help you remember the different steps that you take when you want to accomplish something."

"So all I have to do is to follow those steps?" said Pooh.

"Yes, Pooh," said The Stranger.

"And that's all?" asked Pooh again, slowly.

"Well, there is more that you should know before you start," said The Stranger. "And I would be very happy to show you. But, basically, yes, that is all you need to know."

"Oh, good! We're ready!" squeaked Roo, who then ran about in circles twice before controlling himself and sitting down again.

"But there is just one small thing," said The Stranger.

"I should have known," moaned Eeyore. "Just when everything looked rosy, bright, and 'Here we go gathering nuts in May' . . . I should have known."

"And it is that—" said The Stranger.

"Uh, excuse me," said Pooh. "Just one small question first. Uh . . . just exactly what is it that we will be successful at?"

"Very good, Pooh!" said The Stranger. "That is just what I was going to talk about. And that is, what is Success?"

"Success is knowing the answers in school," said Piglet, who had gone to school in Christopher Robin's pocket, but who had not known many answers when he was there.

"Success is being known," said Pooh, although he wasn't quite sure that that was all there was to it.

"Success is a large field of thistles," said Eeyore.

"Or playing in a large Sandy Pit," said Roo.

"That's very interesting," said The Stranger. "But I think you'll agree that one thing that we found out was that each of you has explained it differently."

"Is that bad?" asked Eeyore.

"It's not bad. But it is important to understand," said The Stranger. "Each of us defines success in his or her own way. Piglet said success was knowledge, and Pooh said that it was fame—"

"I did?" said Pooh.

"—Eeyore said that success was fortune, in the way of a large field of thistles, and Roo said that success was just being. No one answer is either right or wrong, as each is right for each one of you. A dictionary definition of success might say 'achieving a desired result,' but this definition includes the thought that success is personal to the individual who defines what result is desired."

"So the Success Formula helps with that?" asked Piglet.

"Yes," said The Stranger. "It can direct your personal growth, or your spiritual growth, and help you to accomplish those things that are most important to you."

"Personally, I think I've grown enough," said Eeyore.

"What if you don't know?" asked Pooh. "If you've grown enough, that is. Or if being known is enough."

"It helps you to decide what result you desire," said The Stranger, "and it helps you to achieve that result. Whether you are working on Wall Street or searching for enlightenment—realigning your spiritual morality or trying to enjoy the present—whether you are a businessman or a bear, a student or a—"

"Piglet!" shouted Piglet.

"—or a piglet. Whether you are interested in improving your work, getting a new job, or creating a full-time job out of a hobby, the process for defining what success means to you, and then setting out and achieving that result, is the same."

"That's all very nice," said Pooh. "But it is usually the 'Hows' that I have trouble with."

"Let me tell you a story," said The Stranger. "Perhaps it will help to explain the process to you."

And he began to tell about the time that Pooh discovered the North Pole. And though they all remembered just what had happened, it was enjoyable to be sitting in the warm sunshine and hearing about it all over again.

Christopher Robin was sitting outside his door, putting on his Big Boots. As soon as he saw the Big Boots,

Pooh knew that an Adventure was going to happen, and he brushed the honey off his nose with the back of his paw, and spruced himself up as well as he could, so as to look Ready for Anything.

"Good-morning, Christopher Robin," he called out.

"Hallo, Pooh Bear. I can't get this boot on."

"That's bad," said Pooh.

"Do you think you could very kindly lean against me, 'cos I keep pulling so hard that I fall over backwards."

Pooh sat down, dug his feet into the ground, and pushed hard against Christopher Robin's back, and Christopher Robin pushed hard against his, and pulled and pulled at his boot until he had got it on.

"And that's that," said Pooh. "What do we do next?"

"We are all going on an Expedition," said Christopher Robin, as he got up and brushed himself. "Thank you, Pooh."

"Going on an Expotition?" said Pooh eagerly. "I don't think I've ever been on one of those. Where are we going to on this Expotition?"

"Expedition, silly old Bear. It's got an 'x' in it."

"Oh!" said Pooh. "I know." But he didn't really.

"X-words are very difficult, you know," said Pooh.

"Exceptionally," said Owl.

"We're going to discover the North Pole."

"Oh!" said Pooh again. "What *is* the North Pole?" he asked.

"It's just a thing you discover," said Christopher Robin carelessly, not being quite sure himself.

"Oh! I see," said Pooh. "Are bears any good at discovering it?"

"Of course they are. And Rabbit and Kanga and all of you. It's an Expedition. That's what an Expedition means. A long line of everybody. You'd better tell the others to get ready, while I see if my gun's all right. And we must all bring Provisions."

"Bring what?"

"Things to eat."

"Oh!" said Pooh happily. "I thought you said Provisions. I'll go and tell them." And he stumped off.

"When Pooh saw the big boots," The Stranger explained to the group of animals around him, "Pooh knew that Christopher Robin felt like having an adventure. This was an example of the step 'Select a Dream.' That is, Christopher Robin had decided the general direction or idea of something that he wanted to do.

"When he told Pooh that they were going on an expedition—"

"Expotition," corrected Pooh.

"—Christopher Robin had used his dream of having an adventure to 'Set the Goal' of finding the North

Pole. The next step, 'Create a Plan,' was accomplished as all of you began to prepare and get ready for the expedition. Getting a long line of everybody together and going to discover the North Pole were parts of the plan. Another part of the plan was to bring provisions—"

"And Christopher Robin's gun," said Piglet. "In case of Woozles and Heffalumps, you know."

"—and to do this you needed to 'Consider Resources,'" said The Stranger, "and make sure you had enough of all the different things that you thought you might need."

"But what about the next step?" asked Piglet. "The one that's called 'Enhance Skills and Abilities.' Does that have something to do with Kanga's Strengthening Medicine?"

"No," said The Stranger. "When—"

"Oh, that's good," said Piglet, who then shivered, remembering how awful it had tasted.

"—we say 'Enhance Skills and Abilities,' we're talking about improving or gaining skills that you think will be needed to achieve the goal you have set for yourself. Like Pooh was doing before the Expedition. Do you remember?"

And The Stranger told them about what had happened with Pooh before the Expedition.

One fine day Pooh had stumped up to the top of the Forest to see if Christopher Robin was interested in Bears at all. At breakfast that morning (a simple meal of marmalade spread lightly over a honeycomb or two) he had suddenly thought of a new song. It began like this:

"Sing Ho! for the life of a Bear!"

When he had got as far as this, he stretched his head and thought to himself "That's a very good start for a song, but what about the second line?" He tried singing "Ho," two or three times, but it didn't seem to help. "Perhaps it would be better," he thought, "if I sang Hi for the life of a Bear." So he sang it . . . but it wasn't. "Very well, then," he said, "I shall sing that first line twice, and perhaps if I sing it very quickly, I shall find myself singing the third and fourth lines before I have time to think of them, and that will be a Good Song. Now then:"

> Sing Ho! for the life of a Bear!
> Sing Ho! for the life of a Bear!
> I don't much mind if it rains or snows,
> 'Cos I've got a lot of honey on my nice
> new nose,
> I don't much care if it snows or thaws,
> 'Cos I've got a lot of honey on my nice
> clean paws!
> Sing Ho! for a Bear!
> Sing Ho! for a Pooh!
> And I'll have a little something in an hour
> or two!

He was so pleased with this song that he sang it all the way to the top of the Forest, "and if I go on singing it much longer," he thought, "it will be time for the little something, and then the last line won't be true." So he turned it into a hum instead.

"Practicing your humming was a very good way to improve your skills," said The Stranger. "And it's just the kind of thing we are talking about when we say, 'Enhance Skills and Abilities.' This step is part of the process that allows you to do things that you may never have done before. By acquiring new skills, or improving skills you already have, it enables you to accomplish things that you may have thought impossible."

"Like making up my North Pole song during the Expotition," said Pooh.

"When you, Pooh, met Rabbit," said The Stranger, "and asked him to relay the message about the forming of the expedition to Kanga, you were delegating the task of telling others to Rabbit, which was a good example of how to 'Spend Time Wisely,' the next step in the Success Formula."

That kind of Bear, thought Pooh. "Which part was that exactly?" he said.

The Stranger told that part of the story:

"Hallo, Rabbit," he said, "is that you?"

"Let's pretend it isn't," said Rabbit, "and see what happens."

"I've got a message for you."

"I'll give it to him."

"We're all going on an Expotition with Christopher Robin!"

"What is it when we're on it?"

"A sort of boat, I think," said Pooh.

"Oh! that sort."

"Yes. And we're going to discover a Pole or something. Or was it a Mole? Anyhow we're going to discover it."

"We are, are we?" said Rabbit.

"Yes. And we've got to bring Po—things to eat with

us. In case we want to eat them. Now I'm going down to Piglet's. Tell Kanga, will you?"

In a little while they were all ready at the top of the Forest, and the Expotition started. First came Christopher Robin and Rabbit, then Piglet and Pooh; then Kanga, with Roo in her pocket, and Owl; then Eeyore; and, at the end, in a long line, all Rabbit's friends-and-relations.

"I didn't ask them," explained Rabbit carelessly. "They just came. They always do. They can march at the end, after Eeyore."

"And so you see," said The Stranger, "you all performed the last step admirably. That step is 'Start! Get Organized and Go.' And you did!"

"Yes," said Piglet. "But that was just the beginning. All kinds of things happened after that."

"That's right, Piglet," said The Stranger. "Adventures are just like that. But it is the beginnings of things that most have a problem with, and you got a very good beginning and were most successful."

"Yes," squeaked Roo. "Pooh found the North Pole!"

"Now that you've told us all about it," said Pooh after a moment, "I think I'm still confuzzled."

"Me too!" said Piglet.

"It's not easy," said Eeyore.

"But that's just it," said The Stranger. "It is quite easy, if you take it step by step. As a matter of fact, many of the steps are things that you already know how to do."

"Really?" said Pooh.

"Yes," said The Stranger. "For example, Piglet, do you remember one day when Pooh said to you, 'I have decided to catch a Heffalump'?"

"Oh, yes, I do," said Piglet, who shivered again.

"Well that was an example of the second step, where a goal is set."

"But what was the dream that was used?" asked Eeyore.

"I had a dream about a Heffalump," said Pooh.

"I had a horrible nightmare about a Heffalump," squeaked Piglet.

"I'm sure Pooh was thinking of having an adventure," said The Stranger. "Another example was during the Search for Small, you made up a list of the Order of Looking for Things, which is a very fine example of how to 'Create a Plan.' Or when Pooh was counting his pots of honey, which is a good example of how you might 'Consider Resources.' "

"But just *how* will all of this help you to be successful?" asked Pooh.

"By doing the steps of the Success Formula one after the other," said The Stranger, "you are focusing your attention and directing your efforts in an integrated way that is very powerful and useful."

"Useful for what?" asked Pooh.

"To accomplish what you've decided is important to you," said The Stranger. "And this conscious direction of your will is much more powerful than the barriers and constraints that normally keep you from succeeding. And *that* is how it will help you to be successful."

Pooh nodded, though he wasn't quite sure that berries had ever kept him from succeeding, even if complaints sometimes had.

After a moment, The Stranger continued. "And all of the steps are things that are very easy to learn or that you already know. It is using them together that makes them so much more effective. Like when you were counting your honey jars," The Stranger said, indicating Pooh. "That is an example of the fourth step, 'Consider Resources.' "

"That reminds me . . ." said Pooh.

"So you can see," said The Stranger, "that many of these things that are parts of the Success Formula are things that you know how to do already."

"It has got quite late," said Pooh. "Don't you think?"

"But by doing them in the correct order," continued The Stranger, "and by having your dreams and setting your goals consciously, you can accomplish anything you set out to do."

"It must be well past Elevenses," said Pooh. "Nearly Twelveses, I should think."

The Stranger realized that Pooh would be quite unable to concentrate unless something were done, so he unpacked a small snack that he had hurriedly packed when Owl had found him, and they all shared some of it. The Stranger sat back on the railing, which again sagged and cracked ominously, but held. It was only after all of the food was gone and they were sitting and listening to the birds and other sounds of the Forest that Pooh spoke again.

"Everything you have told us is very interesting," he said, "but, being a Bear of Very Little Brain, I need to know more. Do you think you might consider—"

"Yes! Yes!" squealed Piglet. "Stay and teach us more about Success! Please! Please!"

"Well," said The Stranger, "I am very flattered that you have asked me. But I do have a great many things to do and—"

"But we helped *you*," said Pooh, "when you wanted to write your book on Management."

"And then again when you wanted to write about Problem Solving," said Piglet.

"Please," said Roo, tugging The Stranger's trouser leg.

The Stranger thought for a moment and then said, "You are absolutely right. You have been most helpful to me, and if you would like me to stay and teach you about the Success Formula, I shall."

With this, The Stranger jumped down off of the railing where he had been sitting. There was another cracking sound, this one a little louder than the last.

Eeyore walked over to where The Stranger had

been sitting and tested the railing with one foot. Then he leaned against it gently with both front feet. The wood cracked softly, but held. "I was sure that this was going to—" *Crack!* and Eeyore fell off the bridge and into the river.

Pooh and the others rushed over to see if he was all right, but by the time they arrived at the edge of the bridge where the railing used to be, Eeyore had floated underneath the bridge. So everyone rushed to the other side of the bridge and waited.

"There!" shouted Piglet. "There he is!"

And out floated Eeyore, on his back with his four feet sticking up in the air.

"Eeyore," said Pooh. "Are you all right?"

"About as fine as one could be . . . considering," said Eeyore. "I think I have just *succeeded* in becoming a Poohstick again."

"Perhaps we should begin Hooshing," said Pooh.

"No Hooshing!" said Eeyore.

It took a few minutes for all of them to hurry down-river, with The Stranger and Pooh going on this side of the river, and Piglet and Owl on the other, as they didn't know which side Eeyore would float toward. In the end he came ashore on the side with Pooh and The Stranger, and while Owl flew across to help, Piglet had to run all the way back up to the bridge to cross and then back down to where a wet and bedraggled Eeyore was just drying off.

"I don't suppose anyone thinks of success as falling off a bridge," said Eeyore. "I suppose I shall need to learn about success too."

"Well, if we are going to begin learning about Success," said The Stranger, "then I shall need to go and get a room at the Inn in the village, and we can start tomorrow. Does that sound all right? And tomorrow we can start off with the first step, 'Select a Dream.'"

"I shall go home," said Pooh, "and I shall take a nap and have some dreams. Just so that I shall have some dreams to select from, you see." And he did.

II

IN WHICH Selecting a Dream
Is Discussed,
Hows Are Spelled Out,
Horrible Heffalumps
Are Mentioned, and Owl Says
a Few Wise Things

When The Stranger returned the next day, he found
that Pooh, Piglet, Eeyore, Owl, and Roo had been
joined by Tigger, Kanga, Rabbit, and his friends-and-
relations. They had heard that he had returned to the
Hundred Acre Wood.

Pooh was anxious to begin. "What is the first thing
we should do to become a success?" Pooh asked The
Stranger. "I like to begin at the beginning. I get less
confuzzled that way."

"The first thing one must do," said The Stranger
emphatically, "is to decide exactly what it is you
want to accomplish. Once you have done that, Achiev-

ing Your Dream, whatever it might be, becomes easier."

"That's very good to know," said Pooh. "I rather like things that become easier as you go on." He paused and scratched his head thoughtfully. "It has been my experience that most things get more and more difficult as they go on."

The others, gathered together around The Stranger, nodded their agreement. In fact, Eeyore nodded so vigorously that he lost the mouthful of thistle that he had been chewing.

"Keeping my tail attached was easy at first, but lately it's got harder and harder," Eeyore said wearily. "Point proven."

"Not necessarily," said Owl. "There is a saying that practice makes perfect. That implies that the more frequently one does something the better one will get at it and therefore the easier it will become to carry out whatever it is one is attempting to do. When I was very young, flying was not easy. But by practicing and developing my Necessary Dorsal Muscles, I reached my present degree of accomplishment."

Owl twisted his head around to look at Eeyore, who had walked after the thistle he had lost.

"Quod Erat demonstrative," Owl said firmly. "That's Latin, you know."

At this Pooh perked up. "I know something about Latin," he said. "I once had a book written about me in Latin. Whatever Latin is."

The Stranger felt that things were getting away from him quite rapidly. "I think I can show you how the step 'Select a Dream' can make your dream easier to achieve. First, however, can anyone tell me what a dream is?"

"It's when you are asleep," said Piglet, "and it seems that a large Horrible Heffalump is chasing you and you can't get away no matter how fast you run and Pooh is nowhere around to help and Christopher Robin is in school and the Heffalump is getting closer and closer. . . ."

Piglet ran out of breath and had to stop.

"I once had a dream like that," said Pooh. "But the

Heffalump was eating all my honey. Actually, five hundred and eighty-seven Heffalumps were eating my honey." Pooh had to stop, being overcome at remembering that dream. "That's not the kind of a dream I'd want to select," he said.

"The dreams you are both talking about," said Owl, "are a sequence of images passing through a sleeping individual's mind. Somehow, I don't think that is the kind of dream that is under consideration."

"You are right, Owl," said The Stranger. "I am defining 'Dream' as a 'fond hope.' As something you would really like to accomplish, or something you

would like to do. Possibly even an occupation that an individual would like to follow."

"I remember that Christopher Robin used to recite a poem about that," said Rabbit. "It went like this, I think":

Tinker, Tailor,
Soldier, Sailor,
Rich Man, Poor Man,
Ploughboy,
Thief—

Tinker, Tailor,

Soldier, Sailor,

Rich Man, Poor Man,

Ploughboy, Thief—

And what about a Cowboy,
Policeman, Jailer,
Engine-Driver,
Or Pirate Chief?
What about a Postman—or a Keeper at the Zoo?
What about the Circus Man who lets the people through?
And the man who takes the pennies for the round-abouts
and swings,
Or the man who plays the organ, and the other man who
sings?
What about a Conjuror with rabbits in his pockets?
What about a Rocket Man who's always making rockets?
Oh there's such a lot of things to do and such a lot to be.

"I remember that," concluded Rabbit. "Because it's about me."

"Very good," said The Stranger. "You and your relations—"

"Helping a Magician," added Rabbit.

"That's a good example," The Stranger went on. "Because there are lots of things that we can do and be. We need to think about what would please us the most. If we then can achieve it, we would be successful. But each individual must define what success means to him or her. You see, different individuals often have different ideas of what success is. What would satisfy one individual might not meet another's desires, wishes, or dreams."

"I don't see," said Piglet, "how I decide what would please me the most."

"Well, it isn't easy," explained The Stranger, "simply because there are so many choices. One way is to think about what you would like best, what your dream is, without even thinking about what obstacles might keep you from achieving it."

"Tiggers are good at climbing over obstacles," said Tigger, although he wasn't quite certain what an "obstacles" might be.

Pooh, who had gotten distracted by Rabbit's recitation of the poem, asked Owl, "What did The Stranger say?"

"He said," Owl answered, "that you should select an aspiration that is appealing without regard to the constraints of current reality."

"I don't see what perspiration has to do with it," said Pooh.

"Genius. That's what it is," said Eeyore. "Ninety-nine percent perspiration."

Owl peered sternly at Pooh, seeing that he still had a puzzled expression on his face. "Pay attention, Pooh. And you too, Eeyore. He said think about what you like best. Don't worry now whether achieving it might not be practical."

"Oh," said Pooh. "I remember talking about that to Christopher Robin. We were walking along in the Forest and it went like this, as I remember."

"What do you like doing best in the world, Pooh?"

"Well," said Pooh, "what I like best—" and then he had to stop and think. Because although Eating Honey *was* a very good thing to do, there was a moment just before you began to eat it which was better than when you were, but he didn't know what it was called. And then he thought that being with Christopher Robin was a very good thing to do, and having Piglet near was a very friendly thing to have; and so, when he had thought it all out, he said, "What I like best in the whole world is Me and Piglet going to see You, and You saying 'What about a little something?' and Me saying, 'Well, I shouldn't mind a little something, should you, Piglet,' and it being a hummy sort of day outside, and birds singing."

"I like that too," said Christopher Robin.

The Stranger had been listening carefully while Pooh spoke, and when Pooh finished, he nodded his head. "That's a good example, Pooh. It shows the right way to go about selecting your dream that you want to achieve."

"It does?" said Pooh, very much surprised.

"Yes." The Stranger nodded. "You didn't take the first thing you thought of. You measured it against what you thought you might like best, evaluated it, and then altered it and reevaluated it until it met all of your requirements and felt right."

"I—didn't—know—that—I—did—all—that," said Pooh slowly. "I think I only stopped and thought."

"That is what you did, Pooh," agreed The Stranger. "But the thinking process was made up of the individual steps of origination, consideration, measurement, evaluation, alteration, reevaluation, and decision."

"That sounds a lot like something Owl would say," said Pooh. "It sounds very difficult. I didn't know that I could do all those things that you said."

"All of us can, and most of us do," said The Stranger. "It's just that we often do them in a vague sort of offhand way. We think, 'Someday I'd like to travel' or 'Wouldn't it be great if I didn't have to work at this job I have' or 'I'd like to be a movie star' or 'I'd like to lose some weight.' "

Pooh nodded emphatically, thinking about his neglected stoutness exercises that he was supposed to do every morning in front of the glass.

"The thought comes into our mind," The Stranger continued, "but then, because we don't make our dreams concrete and specific or do anything about them, they remain just dreams. Insubstantial, in the  clouds. Our Success Formula is specifically designed to put foundations under them and put us on the road to achieving them, whatever the dreams may be."

"Oh," said Pooh, thinking that might be the reason his stoutness didn't get any less.

The Stranger looked around to each member of the group. "Has everyone here had the kind of dreams we've just been talking about? The sort of 'I wish that—' dreams."

There was silence as everyone thought. Then they all nodded their heads in agreement, except for Alexander Beetle, whose head was stuck in a crack in the forest floor, so his other end nodded instead.

"Good. Then we can all select the dreams that we would like to achieve. Before we do that, there are three points I need to make. When picking out your dreams, don't consider that they may be too difficult to achieve. Second, don't worry that they may be too ambitious. We never know what we can accomplish until we try. Finally, don't be afraid of what others may think about your selection. These are *your* dreams. You are the *only* one who knows what you need to achieve to be successful."

"I still don't see how one decides," said Piglet.

"Yes," Pooh agreed. "Suppose there are two dreams that someone has and they both seem like they would be Very Good to be a success at being. It seems to me that would be Very Bothering. It's like deciding which pot of honey to eat."

"You both have a good point," said The Stranger. "We are all apt to find ourselves in that situation from time to time. Making decisions is often difficult. There are several things you can do to help you select what dream to pursue. You can list the advantages and disadvantages of each. You could even flip a coin to see which to pick. Not that I would recommend that, but after you have flipped the coin, see how you feel about the result. If you don't feel good about the result of the coin toss, then that dream is not for you. You can also think about which dream might take the longest time to achieve and then select the one that takes the least time. You can also try to talk to individuals who have achieved a similar dream and see what they can tell you. Often, gathering more information and facts about what the achievement of the dream might mean will help you to make up your mind. This is not to say that you can't have several dreams that you are interested in and working toward. Perhaps you have a dream about your work, and one that relates to a hobby, and maybe even another concerning something else you are interested in. There is nothing but the limitations on your time and resources that prevents you from having multiple dreams, although we will generally be talking about one dream for the sake of our discussion. You should also remember that you can always adjust and change your dream as you go along.

"Any questions?" The Stranger waited until he was certain that no one had any. "Now, what I would like you to do is to think about how you would answer a question like the one that Christopher Robin asked Pooh. 'What would you like to do best in the world?' Stop and think about what your answer would be just like Pooh did. Take some time between now and, say, tomorrow to come up with your answer so we can begin the process of achieving your dreams."

"One I could achieve right now," said Pooh, "would be to have a little something to prepare me for thinking, which is sometimes difficult to do if one's insides are rumbling, which happens when there has been too long a time since the last little something."

"I think we can take care of that," said The Stranger, turning to a basket he had brought. "We'll all have a little something, then we'll think, and when we meet to-morrow we'll learn how to use our dreams to set a goal."

"Where should we meet?" asked Tig-ger, remembering all the trouble they had

had once before when they had forgotten to set a specific meeting place.

"I know the perfect place," said Pooh, trying to see what was in the basket The Stranger had brought. "Let's meet at the stream by the Big Stones and Rocks."

"That's fine with me," said The Stranger, and all the others agreed as they began to unpack the basket and have a little something.

III

In which Pooh and The Stranger
Are Stuck, Everyone Sets Goals,
and Alexander Beetle Begins
to ACHIEVE One

As he strolled along enjoying the early-morning sun-
light and the songs of early-morning birds looking for
early-morning worms, Pooh was wondering if The
Stranger would think that his dream of having a lot of
honey, say ten or twelve pots every day, was suitable
for being a goal—or if he would have to change it to
five or six pots. The more he thought about it, the more
he was certain that no Thoughtful Person would consider that ten or twelve pots of honey each day was
unreasonable, but perhaps five or six would do, along
with several tins of condensed milk. . . .

He expressed this thought to Piglet, who had by
then caught up and was now strolling along beside him
on their way to their meeting with The Stranger to
learn about Success.

After some thought, Piglet agreed, and they walked

along in silence for a while, Pooh trying to decide if ten or twelve was a better number to use and Piglet just walking.

Pooh had just decided that fifteen was better than either ten or twelve, and that condensed milk wouldn't do at all, when his concentration was spoiled by someone calling his name.

"Pooh. Piglet. Oh, Pooh! Wait for me!"

Pooh turned around. It was The Stranger, trying to untangle himself from the embrace of a thistle.

"Hallo there. Can I help you?" Pooh asked politely.

The Stranger gave a mighty tug and managed to break free. "This is very rough country, Pooh. How did you happen to think of the Big Stones and Rocks as a place to meet? I wondered about it last night, but forgot to ask you."

"Well," said Pooh, sitting down, "you said that we would be talking about Success and Setting Goals and that is where we went when Christopher Robin said our goal was to discover the North Pole." Pooh looked down modestly. "Which I did. Found the North Pole, that is. Me, I mean."

"I see," said The Stranger, nodding thoughtfully. "That seems very reasonable, once you explain it."

"I thought so," said Pooh.

Just at that moment, the bushes beyond a large tree trembled and Eeyore stepped out.

"Hallo, Eeyore," said Pooh and Piglet at the same time.

"Good morning, Eeyore," said The Stranger.

"I suppose so," said Eeyore. "Although it would be much better if one had had breakfast."

"There's a very fine thistle here that The Stranger just got attacked by which might help make up for a lack of breakfast," said Pooh, moving over to where it was to show Eeyore, and tripping and falling into the thistle himself.

Eeyore and The Stranger helped Pooh extricate himself. "Thistles are better if individuals don't thrash about in them before someone has them for breakfast," said Eeyore gloomily. "But thrashed-on thistle is better than none, I suppose."

As Eeyore munched, The Stranger and Pooh removed stickers from various Hard-to-Reach places. Then they helped each other with stickers that were in Impossible-to-Reach locations. Unless you had help, which they did, fortunately. Finally, they finished and set off to follow the nearby stream to the meeting place.

At length they came to the Big Stones and Rocks without slipping into the stream even once. The others were all there waiting for them, even Kanga, Roo, Rabbit, and some of his friends-and-relations.

After all the "Hallos" and "Good mornings" had been said, and Eeyore had finished his thistle, everyone settled in a semicircle. Everyone, that is, except Tigger, who bounced around, trying to pick out a place to sit. The Stranger stood with his back to the stream and the Big Stones and Rocks over which it tumbled. He finally decided to squeeze in next to Piglet, which made Piglet wish that he had chosen another place. Piglet considered moving over next to Pooh, but by then The Stranger had started to talk, so he only moved as far out of the way of a possible sudden, uncontrollable bounce as he could.

"Today we are going to talk about how to 'Use Your Dreams to Set a Goal,'" The Stranger began. "Can anyone tell me what a Goal is?"

"Honey," said Pooh definitely. "Having a lot, that is."

"Heffalumps," said Piglet. "Not meeting them. In the dark, that is."

"Those both could be goals or, for that matter,

dreams," said The Stranger, "but what I wanted was a definition of the word 'goal.' "

Everyone turned and looked at Owl, who was best at that sort of thing, if you left out Christopher Robin, which you had to do because he wasn't there.

"A goal is the result or achieve-ment toward which effort is di-rected. Or," Owl continued, "it could be the posts between which a ball is driven in certain games." Owl peered closely at The Stran-ger, quite impressed with himself.  "Somehow I believe that you might prefer the first definition."

"Exactly right, Owl. In fact, your definition that a goal is the result or achievement toward which effort is directed is just perfect for our purposes of learning about setting goals and the part that that process should play in pursuing and achieving success."

"Why?" asked Roo, who was just at the age when he asked that about almost everything.

"Now, Roo," said Kanga. "I'm certain The Stranger is about to tell us that."

"Why do we set goals?" repeated Roo, delighted that there was someone new to ask. Some of those in the forest became impatient after the seventy-eleventh repetition of "Why?"

At the same time Pooh said, "How do you set a goal?"

"Good questions, both of them. Let's see if I can answer them." The Stranger scratched his head and thought for a moment and then began:

"We set goals because that gives us the best chance of achieving what we 'really' want out of our life and our work. You see, everyone has things that they like and things that they don't like."

"Tiggers don't like honey, but they do like Extract of Malt," offered Tigger.

"Exactly," said The Stranger. "The object is to get more of what you like and less of what you don't like."

"Like Honey," said Pooh dreamily, almost certain that it must be time for elevenses.

"Often, little thought goes into the setting of goals. They just sort of come up and are sometimes acted upon and sometimes not. If you don't set your own goals, you may find yourself doing things that don't excite you, that aren't really important to you, and that don't contribute to your pursuit and achievement of success. You can find yourself not making progress, drifting, treading water."

"I treaded water once when I was surrounded by water during the Flood," volunteered Pooh. "It really wasn't a very nice thing."

"I remember that adventure," said The Stranger. "In the sense I was using that phrase, I meant that you

are not making any progress in achieving what you want and need."

"Oh," said Pooh. "I thought you meant really."

"In addition to not achieving what you want," The Stranger continued, "if you are without goals, it is quite likely that goals will be selected for you. They will be goals by default or goals that are selected from sources outside yourself. These may or may not be what you really want. Goals are often selected for you by your parents, your boss, your partners, your country or government, your society or culture, and so on. One of the things that is bad about having others set goals for you is that you may not be very interested in achieving them or you might not even realize that others have set a goal for you. This can disappoint those who set the goal. Can anyone think of a case where this happened?"

"That happened when we had a goal of trying to unbounce Tigger," said Rabbit.

"Tell us about it."

"Well," said Rabbit, "we had lost our way—and Tigger—in the fog at the top of the Forest."

When Tigger had finished waiting for the others to catch him up, and they hadn't, and when he had got tired of having nobody to say, "I say, come on" to, he thought he would go home. So he trotted back; and the first thing Kanga said when she saw him was "There's a good Tigger. You're just in time for your Strengthening Medicine," and she poured it out for him. Roo said proudly, "I've *had* mine," and Tigger swallowed his and said, "So have I," and then he and Roo pushed each other about in a friendly way, and Tigger accidentally knocked over one or two chairs by accident, and Roo accidentally knocked over one on purpose, and Kanga said, "Now then, run along."

"Where shall we run to?" asked Roo.

"You can go and collect some fir-cones for me," said Kanga, giving them a basket.

So they went to the Six Pine Trees, and threw fir-cones at each other until they had forgotten what they came for, and they left the basket under the trees and went back to dinner.

Rabbit finished, and Roo looked anxiously around to see if anyone would blame him for not having completed the goal of collecting fir-cones for Kanga even though that had happened before he knew what a goal was.

The Stranger noticed Roo doing this and reassured him. "That's a good example, Rabbit. When others set our goals for us, it is difficult to take them as seriously as we do the ones we set for ourselves. So that is the reason we should set goals for ourselves. It gives you the best chance of achieving what you really want. Does that answer your question, Roo?"

Roo nodded, quickly, because everyone was looking at him, which hadn't happened since the time he had fallen into the stream.

"Does everyone understand why we set goals?" The Stranger asked, looking around the half circle.

Everyone nodded, even Alexander Beetle.

"Good," The Stranger continued. "Now, let me explain the 'How' of setting goals. Actually, it is very easy. All of us have dreams that we express as goals. Most of us have been setting goals all our life, even though we may not have thought of it in just that way.

"Some goals that individuals set are:

Get a good grade in the next exam at school.

Win the next game that is played.

Get a raise at the next salary review.

Change occupations.

Lose five pounds.

Send the children to college.

Restore a classic car.

Get an advanced degree.

Retire early.

Improve skills.

Start a business.

Travel to a foreign country.

Do more volunteer work."

The Stranger paused. "The list is endless and I could go on for days. Can any of you give us an example of a dream that you'd like to turn into a goal?"

"Have lots of honey," said Pooh quickly, hoping that it would remind The Stranger that it was surely time for lunch and that they must have gone past elevenses so the lunch should have elevenses added onto it. Just to be fair. "Always."

"To be a good public speaker," said Alexander Beetle, but nobody heard him or paid any attention. This embarrassed him so much that he buried himself head downward behind a thistle until he could recover.

"Not to meet a Horrible Heffalump when I'm by myself," said Piglet.

"To be a better swimmer," piped up Roo.

"To have thistles that are closer to my house," said Eeyore. "It's not very much of a goal, but there you are."

"To be able to bounce better," said Tigger.

Piglet shuddered.

"I think I'd like to change my goal," said Piglet. "If you can do that."

"Absolutely, Piglet," said The Stranger. "Goals should not be cast in concrete or chiseled in stone."

"Or Rocks!" shouted Piglet, his ears twitching with excitement.

"They should be selected after careful thought," continued The Stranger, "but then they should be reviewed regularly to see if they still are what you would like to achieve. We all change with the passing of time and the changing of conditions. When we find that the goals are no longer appropriate or applicable, we need to change them. For instance, your goal of not meeting a Heffalump when you are by yourself will eventually not be very important to you after you have worked out a plan to cope with that eventuality. Then you would want to either change the goal or substitute a new one."

"Thank you," said Piglet. "It's not that the goal is no longer app—whatever you said—but I thought of something else that I wanted to add to it. In addition to not meeting Heffalumps when I'm by myself, I'd also like not to be bounced upon, or sprung at when I'm not expecting it." Piglet looked sternly at Tigger, who didn't seem to notice.

"I'd like to finish reading the encyclopedia," said Owl. "I'm all the way through the B's."

"Now," said The Stranger. "Those are all very good dreams. Think about the ones you have mentioned and the ones I listed. Is there anything that you can think of that might allow us to put them into classes?"

There was silence, except for the bubbling and gurgling of the stream as it passed over and around the Rocks in its bed.

Then Owl spoke up. "If we consider that goals can be classified into categories, we might arbitrarily specify that the duration of time until achievement of the goal is a relevant characteristic in that some of those that have been mentioned will take an extensive amount of time to accomplish, while others might be achieved quite expeditiously."

"Excellent, Owl! That's exactly right."

Piglet leaned over to Rabbit, who usually knew about things, and whispered, "What exactly did Owl say?"

Rabbit thought for a moment. "He said that some goals can be achieved in a hurry and some take a long time."

"That's what I thought," said Piglet. "Thank you, Rabbit."

The Stranger continued. "You see, it is helpful to classify goals as either short-term or long-term by your reasonable estimate of how long it will take to achieve them. Generally, if you think a goal will take six months or less to accomplish, it is a short-term goal. If

it takes longer than that, it is long-term. Some goals can take years to accomplish. Others may take a lifetime. Getting a college degree is an example of a long-term goal."

Pooh was thinking that he hoped that getting honey was a short-term goal. "I still think that I don't understand the 'How' of setting goals quite well enough to do it."

"To turn a dream into a goal," said The Stranger, "all we do is make the dream specific, concrete, and definite. Let me give you an example.

"Let us suppose that it was an individual's dream to become a great actor. In Using the Dream to Set a Goal, the individual would have to decide what kind of actor. Let's say the type of actor he wanted to be was one who acted on stage. The next thing to find out would be what is needed to be a stage actor. By consulting actors and reading books and using other

research methods, the individual would find that a powerful and controlled voice would be required or, in
other words, the individual would want to be a good
public speaker."

Alexander Beetle quickly raised his small head out
of the ground and stood on his hind legs so he could
better see The Stranger over the heads of Rabbit's other
friends-and-relations.

"With further research other requirements would be
found. The ability to memorize lines in a play, knowledge of the history of the theater, attending an actors
studio, knowing how to dance and sing, and so on.

"So, from the dream of wanting to be an actor, the
individual has developed the goal of being a stage actor,
with subgoals of developing a powerful and controlled
speaking voice and an excellent memory, graduating
from an actors studio, learning how to be an adequate
singer and dancer, and whatever else might be required.

"You can see that the dream has taken on sub-
stance. The dream is now a goal, and subgoals have

been established as well. The individual can begin to work on the second part of Owl's definition of deciding how efforts are to be directed to achieve the goal and the subgoals. Work could even begin on one of the subgoals, say developing a powerful and controlled voice, by exercising the lungs and practicing projecting the voice."

"Hooray!" shouted Alexander Beetle. He began to take deep breaths to exercise his lungs.

"What was that?" asked Eeyore, cocking his head to one side. "I thought I heard something. Never mind. I'm often wrong," he said gloomily.

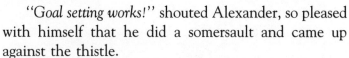

"No," said Pooh. "I distinctly heard something myself."

"Me too," said Piglet, looking at where he thought the sound had come from.

"Goal setting works!" shouted Alexander, so pleased with himself that he did a somersault and came up against the thistle.

"See," said Eeyore. "I heard something again. I think I was right after all."

"I think I understand how to set goals now," said Pooh, "but how do I achieve them?"

"The next step will be to learn how to devise and carry out a plan. We will learn about that the next time we get together since I think we've covered enough today. However, let's summarize the key points of goal setting before we stop for the day.

"Remember that setting goals for yourself gives you the best chance of getting what you 'really' want out of your life and your work. If you don't set your own goals, someone else may set them for you and they may or may not be what you want.

"Now, here are seven things about setting goals we should remember." Rabbit quickly got out a piece of paper and began to write very busily as The Stranger listed the seven items.

All of us have possibility power. Almost anything is possible if we are willing to pay the price. We have much more control over our destiny than we may have realized or exercised in the past.

Choose your goals carefully because *you* are going to achieve them.

Have both long- and short-term goals. As you accomplish them, add new ones.

Imagine accomplishing really ambitious goals. If goals seem intimidating because of the size or time frame of the undertaking, break them down into subgoals that are easier to achieve and that allow you to see the progress you are making to-

ward the ultimate objective. Reward yourself as
you reach each subgoal.

Engendering success requires concrete goals. Be
specific when you establish and write down your
goals.

Value your long-term goals. Don't neglect them in
favor of short-term goals, which may seem easier
to reach. The greatest rewards usually come from
the achievement of long-term goals. If you work
only on the short-term goals, you will never accomplish the long-term goals.

Eliminate conflict between goals. Conflict is natu-
ral and should be expected. Conflicts can be re-
solved by establishing relative priorities, revising
goals, or treating the conflict as a problem and
applying problem-solving techniques.

"Read *Winnie-the-Pooh on Problem Solving*," volunteered Pooh.

"Yes, Pooh," said The Stranger. "I forgot to mention that. Thank you. Next time, as I mentioned, we'll
talk about how we develop Plans to achieve our goals."

"It spells A-C-H-I-E-V-E," said Rabbit, who was
looking at a piece of paper he held.

"What does?" asked Piglet, who hadn't gone to

school with Christopher Robin on days when spelling was being learned.

"I was writing down the seven things that The Stranger said we should remember about goal setting and I just noticed that the first letters of the seven things to remember spell 'achieve,' which is what goal setting helps us to do."

"Oh, good!" said Piglet. "Another acro . . . acro . . . whatever . . . to help us remember."

"Acronym," said Pooh, who had taken particular care to remember the word.

"That's very astute of you, Rabbit," said The Stranger. "I'll use that in my work, if I may."

"Of course," said Rabbit.

"I think we should meet again"—The Stranger thought for a moment—"say Tuesday of next week, to learn about Plans. We covered a great deal of material today and that will give us a chance to think about it. Is that all right with everyone?"

While they all talked about it and then agreed, The Stranger was unpacking his backpack and putting out lots and lots of everyone's favorite food.

"Well," said Pooh, "that's one short-term goal accomplished. There's enough here for elevenses and lunch and some left over for smackerels."

IV

IN WHICH Piglet Makes a Discovery, a Plan Is Created, and Eeyore Is Surprised

The Stranger arrived just when he had said he would and found Pooh, all alone, sitting on a rock in the middle of the stream and humming hums to himself.

"Hallo, Pooh!" said The Stranger. "How are you?"

"Hallo!" said Pooh, jumping up from his place and nearly falling into the water.

"Are the others coming to join us?" asked The Stranger.

"Tigger was here just a moment ago," said Pooh, "but I think he went off chasing a butterfly. He should be back. Owl said he was coming, and I thought Piglet was coming too."

"It certainly is a beautiful day," said The Stranger, admiring the scenery.

"Yes, it is," said Pooh. "What are we going to talk about today?"

"Today we are going to talk about Creating a Plan," said The Stranger.

Pooh scratched his head. "I know I am a Bear of Very Little Brain, but didn't we already learn about Plans? Action Plans? When we were Solving Problems?"

"Quite correct, Pooh!" said The Stranger. "You have more brain than you give yourself credit for. We *did* talk about Action Plans when we were Employing solutions to Problems. And these are exactly the same kinds of things as we discussed then."

"So why do we have to do it again? It being such a nice day and all, and there being so much to do," said Pooh, looking up and down the stream and hoping the others would come along and agree with him. Not that he didn't enjoy talking with The Stranger, but just that it *was* a beautiful day, and there were so many things to do. Like skipping stones a little farther down the river, where if you skipped them just right, they went all the way across. And maybe playing some Poohsticks. And there were certainly enough clouds for playing make-believe.

"If I remember correctly," said The Stranger, "we only discussed Action Plans briefly. Just enough to let us employ our solutions and solve our problems. In this case, as Plans are a Very Important Part of the Success Formula, we shall need to understand them a little better."

"Oh, I wish something exciting would happen," said Pooh, mostly to himself.

"You remember," said The Stranger, "that we started talking about how anyone could do just about anything he wanted if he were to go about it the right way? And how we started by selecting a dream, so we would know where we wanted to go. And then we talked about Using Our Dream to Set a Goal, and how important a step that was. Well, once we have set our goal—"

"I think my new goal is to skip stones," said Pooh, looking downstream to the Skipping Place longingly.

"—the very next thing we do is to Create a Plan to take us there. Remember we said that a goal is a destination—"

"Or maybe my goal is Poohsticks Bridge?" said Pooh.

"—and that you can't *do* a goal. A Plan is our map. It is a list of the things we need to do, in the right order, that will take us from where we are now, to where we want to be."

"I want to be lying on my back in the flowers and staring up at the clouds," sighed Pooh.

"A Plan is a list of things to do," continued The Stranger.

"I wish there was something exciting to do," said Pooh.

At that very moment, there was a loud crashing as

Tigger, preceded by a bright orange-and-yellow butterfly, crashed through the undergrowth next to the stream and flopped to a halt in front of The Stranger and Pooh.

Pooh was about to ask Tigger what he was doing, and The Stranger was about to say hallo, when all three of them heard a tiny squeaky voice calling out as it came nearer.

"Oh! Oh! Pooh! Oh, help, Pooh!"

Piglet came puffing up to where the others were standing, and it was quite some time before he was able to catch his breath. So The Stranger and Pooh and Tigger waited patiently while Piglet tried to control himself.

"I'm so glad . . . huff . . . I thought . . . huff . . . and then I looked . . . huff . . . and then I remembered . . . huff . . . so I ran . . . huff . . . big problem . . . huff . . ." and so on until they were able to calm Piglet down sufficiently so that he could speak.

"Pooh, do you know what day it is today?" asked Piglet.

"It's Tuesday!" shouted Tigger, as he began to bounce up and down in an excited fashion. Piglet moved to the other side of The Stranger, not wanting to get bounced.

"And not just *any* Tuesday," said Piglet. "This is the Tuesday that is also Eeyore's Birthday!"

"Eeyore's Birthday?" said Pooh.

"Yes!" said Piglet. "I was hurrying along to meet you here when I ran into Eeyore—"

"You Bounced him?" said Tigger.

"—and you know how sad he is," continued Piglet, "especially on his birthday, and he told me that this was a special day for him, one that comes only once a year, but then who cares, you know how he can be, and that he didn't really expect much of anything except that if it would rain that would be quite a nice touch, and that he wasn't even expecting anyone to notice or anything, because after all, he's just a donkey."

"What did you say, Piglet?" asked Pooh.

"What could I say?" answered Piglet. "I told him I was on my way to meet you and that I was sure that the others must be too, as they weren't standing there with us and had to be somewhere, and it being a special day for Eeyore, that it was as good a somewhere as any other. Oh, what shall we do, Pooh? You remember how sad he was the last time this happened?"

Pooh said that he remembered, and then went on to tell the story of how he had met Eeyore in the Forest one day. . . .

Eeyore, the old grey Donkey, stood by the side of the stream, and looked at himself in the water.

"Pathetic," he said. "That's what it is. Pathetic."

He turned and walked slowly down the stream for twenty yards, splashed across it, and walked slowly back on the other side. Then he looked at himself in the water again.

"As I thought," he said. "No better from *this* side. But nobody minds. Nobody cares. Pathetic, that's what it is."

There was a crackling noise in the bracken behind him, and out came Pooh.

"Good morning, Eeyore," said Pooh.

"Good morning, Pooh Bear," said Eeyore gloomily. "If it *is* a good morning," he said. "Which I doubt," said he.

"Why, what's the matter?"

"Nothing, Pooh Bear, nothing. We can't all, and some of us don't. That's all there is to it."

"Can't all *what?*" said Pooh, rubbing his nose.

"Gaiety. Song-and-dance. Here we go round the mulberry bush."

"Oh!" said Pooh. . . . "You seem so sad, Eeyore."

"Sad? Why should I be sad? It's my birthday. The happiest day of the year."

"Your birthday?" said Pooh in great surprise.

"Of course it is. Can't you see? Look at all the presents I have had." He waved a foot from side to side. "Look at the birthday cake. Candles and pink sugar."

Pooh looked—first to the right and then to the left.

"Presents?" said Pooh. "Birthday cake?" said Pooh. *"Where?"*

"Can't you see them?"

"No," said Pooh.

"Neither can I," said Eeyore. "Joke," he explained. "Ha ha!"

Pooh scratched his head, being a little puzzled by all this.

"But is it really your birthday?" he asked.

"It is."

"Oh! Well, many happy returns of the day, Eeyore . . ."

"It's bad enough," said Eeyore, almost breaking down, "being miserable myself, what with no presents and no cake and no candles, and no proper notice taken of me at all, but if everybody else is going to be miserable too—"

This was too much for Pooh. "Stay there!" he called to Eeyore, as he turned and hurried back home as quick as he could; for he felt that he must get poor Eeyore a present of *some* sort at once, and he could always think of a proper one afterwards.

"We shall cheer up Eeyore," said Pooh. "We shall celebrate his birthday even more grandly than we did before. Don't you all agree?"

Tigger and Piglet nodded. The Stranger nodded too.

"So what shall we do?" asked Piglet.

"Aha!" said The Stranger. None of the animals had expected an Aha! just then, and they were quite surprised to hear it coming from The Stranger. And it wasn't the type of Aha! that you caught Horrible Heffalumps with, thought Piglet, so it must be something even more important.

"Perhaps I can help," said The Stranger. "Here is a goal you've set for yourself, to prepare a birthday party for Eeyore, and while we are doing that we can learn about Plans. Why, we can even compare this birthday party with Eeyore's other birthday and see if we are successful."

"Oh! Oh! Can I help?" cried Piglet.

"Me too! Me too!" said Tigger, bouncing excitedly and nearly knocking Piglet down.

"Tell us what we must know," said Pooh, "so that we can get started."

"Once we have our goal," said The Stranger, "we must break it down into individual steps. And each step should be simple and straightforward so that we can identify the three elements of each step."

"Did he say Heffalumps?" said Piglet to Pooh, looking very worried.

"The three parts of each Plan step are . . ." continued The Stranger.

"I guess not," said Pooh.

"What. Who. And When."

"That's three of the Five W's!" cried Pooh. "I remember them!"

"That's exactly right, Pooh," said The Stranger. "In this instance they are helping us to create the steps of our Plan instead of helping us to ask questions as they did before. The What stands for 'What is to be done?' The Who means 'Who is going to do it?' And the When is for 'When are they going to do it?'"

"Isn't Who on first?" asked Piglet.

"I beg your pardon?" said The Stranger.

"Something I heard someplace . . . never mind," said Piglet.

"I think Piglet was trying to ask in what order we usually create the steps," said The Stranger. "And the answer is that normally we will want to create all of the Whats—that is, list all of the things that need to be done, and then assign Who will do them and also When they can be accomplished."

"How do we know how many steps we need?" asked Pooh, scratching his head.

"Usually," said The Stranger, "the bigger the goal, the more steps you will need to achieve it."

"I know it takes a lot of steps to go to Owl's house," said Pooh.

"And you should also be aware," said The Stranger,

"that some goals have Plans that will take a long time to accomplish. Especially when we are talking about goals that relate to something like success."

"Why is that?" asked Piglet.

"Because," said The Stranger, "often the goals we set for ourselves are so high. In this case, we can make each part easier and also give ourselves milestones to judge our progress, by breaking the goals down into smaller elements and tasks."

"Did he just mention Heffalumps again?" asked Piglet of Pooh.

"He must have. I heard him say 'tusks' too," said Pooh to Piglet, who was shivering now.

"When we make up our list of steps it is important not to be judgmental, as many of the steps when you are starting out may seem quite difficult or impossible. By the time you reach that step, you will have already accomplished a lot and will have many more capabilities than you had at the beginning. If you arrive at a step and it still seems impossible, you may want to examine it and see if *it* can be broken down into simpler substeps and made easier to do."

"Can we start? Can we start!" said Tigger, as he began bouncing. "Starting is what Tiggers do best!"

"Let's start by reviewing our goal," said The Stranger. "Pooh, can you say it again?"

"Our goal," said Pooh proudly, "is to celebrate

Eeyore's birthday in a better way than last time, and so that he won't be so sad and gloomy."

"Good," said The Stranger. "Now how do we go about doing that?"

"We should wrap all the presents in pretty paper!" cried Piglet.

"But we don't have any presents yet," said Pooh.

"Oh," said Piglet.

"That brings up a very good point," said The Stranger. "When we are making up the list of steps in our Plan, we will find that some of the steps can only be accomplished when another previous step has been completed. Just like here. We can't wrap the presents until we decide what the presents are and get them. So this is a Dependent Step, one that depends on the completion of a prior step. The other, Independent Steps, can usually be done at any time. Do you understand?"

"I think so," said Pooh. "If one of our steps is to help Eeyore eat his birthday cakes, once he's blown out all the candles and made his wishes and everyone has sung to him, we must wait until all that is over before we help him," Pooh finished sadly.

"That's right, Pooh," said The Stranger. "Perhaps now we should remember how the preparations for his last party went."

And so Pooh continued to tell the story of Eeyore's last birthday.

The first thing Pooh did was to go to the cupboard to see if he had quite a small jar of honey left; and he had, so he took it down.

"I'm giving this to Eeyore," he explained, "as a present. What are *you* going to give?"

"Couldn't I give it too?" said Piglet. "From both of us?"

"No," said Pooh. "That would *not* be a good plan."

"All right, then, I'll give him a balloon. I've got one left from my party. I'll go and get it now, shall I?"

"That, Piglet, is a *very* good idea. It is just what Eeyore wants to cheer him up. Nobody can be uncheered with a balloon."

So off Piglet trotted; and in the other direction went Pooh, with his jar of honey.

It was a warm day, and he had a long way to go. He hadn't gone more than half-way when a sort of funny feeling began to creep all over him. It began at the tip of his nose and trickled all through him and out at the soles of his feet. It was just as if somebody inside him were saying, "Now then, Pooh, time for a little something."

"Dear, dear," said Pooh, "I didn't know it was as late as that." So he sat down and took the top off his jar of honey. "Lucky I brought this with me," he thought. "Many a bear going out on a warm day like this would never have thought of bringing a little something with him." And he began to eat.

"Now let me see," he thought, as he took his last lick of the inside of the jar, "where was I going? Ah, yes, Eeyore." He got up slowly.

And then, suddenly, he remembered. He had eaten Eeyore's birthday present!

"Bother!" said Pooh. "What *shall* I do? I *must* give him *something*."

For a little while he couldn't think of anything. Then he thought: "Well, it's a very nice pot, even if there's no honey in it, and if I washed it clean, and got somebody to write 'A *Happy Birthday*' on it, Eeyore could keep things in it, which might be Useful." So, as he was just passing the Hundred Acre Wood, he went inside to call on Owl, who lived there.

"So you see," said The Stranger, "when you found out about Eeyore's birthday you set yourselves the goal of getting a present for him. Pooh, you went home and got him a jar of honey, a very fine present."

"Yes," said Pooh. "It was *very* fine."

"And after you had made sure," laughed The Stranger, "you decided to write 'A Happy Birthday' on it. Which you knew would require you to go to Owl's house, and ask him to write it for you, then wash out the pot and dry it, and have Owl write on it, before you could give it to Eeyore. Those are all steps in the process of achieving the goal of getting a present for Eeyore. Those are all part of your Plan."

"It would have been a lot easier if I hadn't eaten Eeyore's present to begin with," said Pooh.

"Yes," said The Stranger. "However, it does point out the fact that Plans can change as a result of things that happen while you are working on them. And when a change occurs, it can mean that you have more steps to perform, or that some of the steps you have planned may not be required."

"Like what happened with *my* present for Eeyore," squeaked Piglet. And he told some more of the story.

While all this was happening, Piglet had gone back to his own house to get Eeyore's balloon. He held it very tightly against himself, so that it shouldn't blow away, and he ran as fast as he could so as to get to Eeyore before Pooh did; for he thought that he would like to be the first one to give a present, just as if he had thought of it without being told by anybody. And running along, and thinking how pleased Eeyore would be, he didn't look where he was going . . . and suddenly he put his foot in a rabbit hole and fell down flat on his face.

BANG!!!??? ***!!!

Piglet lay there, wondering what had happened. At first he thought that the whole world had blown up; and then he thought that perhaps only the Forest part of it had; and then he thought that perhaps only *he* had, and he was now alone in the moon or somewhere, and would never see Christopher Robin or Pooh or Eeyore again. And then he thought, "Well, even if I'm in the moon, I needn't be face downwards all the time," so he got cautiously up and looked about him.

He was still in the Forest!

"Well, that's funny," he thought. "I wonder what that bang was. I couldn't have made such a noise just falling down. And where's my balloon? And what's that small piece of damp rag doing?"

It was the balloon!

"Oh, dear!" said Piglet. "Oh, dear, oh, dearie, dearie, dear! Well, it's too late now. I can't go back, and I haven't another balloon, and perhaps Eeyore doesn't *like* balloons so *very* much."

"I can see that things changed quite drastically for you, Piglet," said The Stranger.

"Yes," said Piglet sadly, trying to hide himself behind Rabbit because everyone was looking at him.

"Now that we've talked about Plans, let's get to work on *our* Plan," said The Stranger.

The Stranger opened his briefcase and took out his laptop computer and began to type in all of the suggestions that everyone had. They continued adding new ideas and changing ideas that they had, and even eliminating some that repeated other steps they had created.

The Stranger stopped for a moment and held up the list for everyone to see. It looked like this:

Get cakes with pink sugar icing

Wrap presents for Eeyore

Meet at the Six Pine Trees

Sing "Happy Birthday to you"

Tell everyone to meet at the Six Pine Trees

Get presents for Eeyore

Eat the cakes

Give Eeyore his presents

Shout "Surprise!"

Tell Eeyore to come to the Six Pine Trees

"That's a very good start," said The Stranger. "But now we must do even better. We should arrange the list in order of priority and make sure that any Dependent Steps come after the steps they're dependent upon."

"Like we can't eat the cakes until we first get them!" said Pooh.

"And we have to break down any large or complex steps," said The Stranger.

"Like getting presents," said Piglet. "We don't say what the presents are or who is going to get which one."

"Good, Piglet," said The Stranger. "And finally we need to assign responsibilities to the different steps and say when they are going to be done."

"What if they aren't done on time?" asked Pooh. "What if the cakes don't arrive before it is time to eat them?"

"When we're doing an Action Plan," said The Stranger, "we try to anticipate just exactly how long everything will take. Sometimes it's helpful to expect things to take a little longer than you might think, as unexpected things do occur."

"Like balloons bursting," added Piglet.

"Sometimes there is nothing you can do but to revise the timing of the rest of the Plan," said The Stranger. "Or sometimes, one thing will take longer, but you will save time on some other step and catch up with your original schedule. Either way, as long as you watch your plan and do your best, you are moving toward your goal as fast as the situation will allow."

They worked on the Plan for Eeyore's Birthday some more, and soon the list was complete.

Pooh had put only his name under "Eat the cakes," but they all thought it would be polite to share, as it was Eeyore's birthday, after all, and the cakes were

PLAN FOR EEYORE'S BIRTHDAY

What	Who	When
Tell everyone about the party	Tigger	Morning
Get cakes with pink sugar icing	The Stranger	Morning
Presents for Eeyore:		
2 red balloons (in case one bursts)	Piglet	Midday
2 pots of honey (in case one is eaten)	Pooh	Midday
Thistles	Tigger	Midday
Wrap presents for Eeyore	Kanga	Early Afternoon
Meet at the Six Pine Trees	All	Afternoon
Tell Eeyore to come to the Six Pine Trees	Tigger	When all are ready
Shout "Surprise!"	All	When Eeyore arrives

What	Who	When
Sing Happy Birthday	All	After "Surprise!"
Give Eeyore his presents	All	After we sing
Eat the cakes	Pooh, et al.	After Eeyore opens presents

Eeyore's presents, and when The Stranger added "et al." he explained that it was a Latin phrase that meant "and others"—but it sounded to Pooh like "ate it all," so he was happy.

"That is a fine Plan," said The Stranger. "Can anyone think of anything to add to it?"

No one did. And so as Tigger bounced off to let everyone know to meet at the Six Pine Trees, and as The Stranger went off to the village to get cakes at the bakery there, Pooh and Piglet started for home to get their presents for Eeyore.

"Here he comes!" squeaked Piglet.

"Quiet everybody! Sssshhhh!" shushed Pooh.

The figure making its way up toward the small crest where the Six Pine Trees were was hard to make out through the bushes and tree trunks. Everyone was hiding behind the trees, gorse, and heather and ready to spring out and Surprise Eeyore when he arrived.

"Surprise!"

The Stranger nearly dropped the large parcel he was carrying when they all shouted and jumped out from their hiding places.

"Oh, my goodness!" said The Stranger. "That was certainly good practice. If it was my birthday, I should have been very surprised. But Eeyore must be coming along behind me if he's not here already. Sorry I'm late."

The Stranger set his parcel down near all the other presents and took up a position near one of the larger trees.

"He should be along any moment now," said Pooh.

"Unless he's been captured by a Heffalump, that is," added Piglet.

"Are all of the preparations made?" asked The Stranger. "Is everything ready?"

"Oh, yes," said little Roo from his hiding place inside Kanga's pouch. "It's going to be a wonderful party."

They all quieted down when one of Rabbit's friends-and-relations hurried back to the group and whispered, "Here he comes! Here he comes!"

They hid themselves again as the figure moved slowly into the open area surrounding the Six Pine Trees.

"Surprise!"

An astonished Tigger bounced three times as high as a normal bounce and came down quite shaken, saying only, "He—he—he's right behind me. Quick! Hide!"

Another figure slowly entered the clearing, looking this way and that.

"Surprise!"

It was Eeyore.

"Happy birthday, Eeyore!"

"Many Happy Returns of the Day!" said Pooh.

Eeyore looked at everyone gathered in a small circle around him. There was Rabbit, and Kanga (with Roo, of course), and Tigger, and Pooh and Piglet and The Stranger, and he was sure that Alexander Beetle was around somewhere.

"Meaning me?" said Eeyore, after looking behind his tail to make certain no one else was there.

"Of course, Eeyore," said Pooh.

"My birthday?"

"Yes," said Piglet.

"I have something Very Important to say," said Eeyore gloomily.

"Yes, yes! Speech!" they shouted.

"Ahem," said Eeyore. "I'm sorry to say, but then that's just the way things are, that today is *not* my birthday."

"Not your birthday?" asked Pooh.

"No. I would know my birthday," said Eeyore, "and this is not it."

"You're certain?" said Piglet, realizing that he was

the one who had told everyone else that it was. "I thought you said this was a day that comes only once a year. A very special day for donkeys, you said. Not that it matters, as no one will notice anyway, you said."

"That's right, Little Piglet," said Eeyore. "Once a year, every year, whether I need it or not, I take a bath. Not that it makes much difference to the rest of you, but it is a kind of habit I fell into that day we were playing Poohsticks, do you remember, and I have just kept it up. Not that I need Tigger to bounce me, even though that would help sometimes when the water's cold."

Pooh, The Stranger, and the others looked at each other silently and wondered what to do. The cakes were all ready, the presents were all wrapped, and most of all, they were all looking forward to a celebration. What were they going to do?

The silence lengthened.

"Well," said Pooh, "in that case, *Happy Bathday!*"

"Yes," they all said. *"Happy Bathday!"*

"Many Happy Returns of the Day!" said Piglet.

And on the party went. They all sang "Happy Bath-day to You" to Eeyore and had some of the cakes that The Stranger had gotten in the village, the ones with the pink sugar icing, and they watched and laughed as Eeyore opened his presents. It was only after all of the presents were opened, and all of the songs were sung, and speeches made, that they gathered around and things quieted down.

"Hooray for Eeyore on his Bathday!" said Piglet.

"And hooray for Pooh," said Owl, "whoooo-se Very Clever idea it was!"

Pooh smiled broadly. *That* kind of bear!

"And thank you to The Stranger," said Pooh, "for teaching us about Creating Plans, so that we could or-gandise this party for Eeyore and have it be a Success."

"You're most welcome, Pooh," said The Stranger. "I'm so glad we had a chance to practice using our plan as we learned about them. Plans can be very powerful and very useful for getting you organized and directed toward your goals. They allow you to use all of your skills, and the skills and efforts of others. They allow you to keep focused on only those things that need to be done to reach your goal, and they help you to keep track of, and realize, your progress. So remember, a Plan is a list of individual activities that outline the way to get from where you are now to where you want to be."

"Like a topographic cartogram," said Owl.

"Or a map!" squeaked Piglet.

"That is precisely what I said," said Owl.

"Oh," said Piglet.

"And we do this by thinking of all of the possible steps and activities that we need to do to reach our goal. Just like we did for Eeyore's party. Once we have thought of all of the steps we can, we begin by organizing them in priority order, remembering that some steps are independent, and that some are dependent, that they depend on the completion of previous activities. We remember not to be judgmental about the activities we list, for we can take difficult steps and break them down into smaller, easier steps if we are having trouble, and we remember, too, that as we begin our Plan, the situation can change, and that may affect the activities we select. Once we have decided What is to be done, that is, the list of activities, we can then begin to assign Who is to do them. If we are talking about your personal Plan to become successful, it is possible that *you* will be the Who for all of them."

"Who?" said Owl, who had dozed off momentarily.

"The last thing we add to our Plan is the When," The Stranger went on. "For each step of the Plan, we will add the date or time that this step is to be completed. At this point you might want to review your plan to make sure that all of your steps *are* doable, that is, that they are activities and not goals. And that each one has been assigned a person responsible and a time for completion."

"What if you have more than one goal?" asked Pooh. "I often get confuzzled when it's almost Elevenses and I'm on my way to Piglet's house, and in the middle of a hum."

"That's a very good question, Pooh," said The Stranger. "When you use Plans to pursue your goals, you'll find that you can pursue many different goals at the same time. Because you have broken each goal down into specific actions, and because you only need to do whichever action is next on the list, you can be working on several different goals at once. You may have personal goals and professional goals and social goals that you can work on all at the same time."

"But what happens if there's a problem?" asked Piglet.

"That's easy," said Pooh. "We SOLVE it!"

"That's right, Pooh," said The Stranger. "If you run into difficulties, you can use problem solving to help you out. You can break difficult steps down into smaller, easier steps, or perhaps you'll find that there is a different way to do what needs to be done, and you can change the steps in your plan. And don't forget to celebrate your achievements as you progress through your plan. Small rewards along the way will motivate you and help you realize the progress you're making."

"Like Bathday Parties!" squealed Roo.

"Like Bathday Parties," said The Stranger.

They all stayed until all of the cakes were gone and everyone said their good-byes and began to walk home. The Stranger said he would be back soon to talk about resources, which are something like reservoirs, Pooh told Piglet, and that he hoped they would all come along. Finally, just Pooh and Piglet and Eeyore were left standing by the Six Pine Trees.

"Well, Eeyore," said Pooh. "Many happy ret—"

"Typical," interrupted Eeyore. "I've forgotten something."

"I don't think so," said Pooh, looking around. "I told you that I would bring the presents round to your house tomorrow."

"No, Pooh," said Eeyore, "I've forgotten to *do* something."

"What's that?" asked Piglet.

"I forgot to take my bath," said Eeyore gloomily.

 "Typical. I suppose I'll just have to go and have it now. It shouldn't be too cold, even though it is getting late, but then what do you expect. Then again, it could rain. . . ."

Eeyore walked off, still talking to himself.

V

In which The Stranger Isn't Backson, Racehorses Are Considered, and Everyone's Skills Are Inventoried

"Bother!" said Pooh.

Piglet quickly looked over his shoulder to make certain that Heffalumps hadn't crept up on them, as he had heard they were wont to do. Only Roo and Tigger were there, having a quick game of fir-cones while they waited for Something to Happen.

"*Oh, bother!*" said Pooh.

Piglet quickly looked around Pooh, but there wasn't

anything behind Pooh, unless you counted Kanga, fondly watching Roo; Eeyore, who was contentedly munching a thistle; and Owl, who had perched himself on a branch just above. None of them looked the least bit like a Horrible Heffalump, so he decided it was safe to ask Pooh what was bothering him.

"What's the matter, Pooh?"

"I'm trying to remember when The Stranger said he'd be back and what we were going to talk about, and I can't. I fear I'm a Bear of Very Little Brain."

Piglet thought about the last time they had seen The Stranger and what it was that The Stranger had said they would talk about.

"It . . . seems . . . to . . . me . . ." he said slowly, thinking so hard that his forehead wrinkled up and his

 ears bent back, which they usually did only when there was a strong wind blowing.

". . . that he didn't say *when*, but he did say *what* we would talk about."

"That's not right," said Rabbit, who had just joined them. "I remember clearly that The Stranger promised to be 'Backson.'"

"That is my recollection also," agreed Owl. "But I believe he said 'back soon.'"

"And that's why I'm so bothered," said Pooh. "It

seems to me that it must be 'back soon' by now and The Stranger isn't anywhere to be seen."

"Maybe The Stranger got lost," said Rabbit.

"Or, it is conceivable that matters of a Greater Degree of Urgency have occupied The Stranger," said Owl, "so fulfilling the promise of being 'back soon' was impractical."

"Oh! Oh!" squeaked Piglet. "I just remembered what we were to talk about. It was racehorses."

"Of course," said Eeyore, looking up from his thistle. "Of course, a horse. That explains it. The Stranger must be looking for a racehorse. Good ones are very difficult to find and are very expensive. After donkeys, horses are really the only proper subject for a serious discussion." Eeyore paused for a moment to chew reflectively.

"Many don't know that donkeys and horses are related, or they just don't care," he said gloomily. "That's just the way things are. In case anyone cares to know, the family is Equidae. The genus is *Equus*. I am *Equus asinus*. The horse is *Equus caballus*. Like being cousins, you know."

"A horse is a solid-hoofed perissodactyl quadruped," said Owl firmly, settling the matter. "But that is not what The Stranger said we would talk about. The subject was to be 'Resources, to carry out our plan.' Something else entirely."

"I thought it was racehorses," said Piglet.

"So did I," said Pooh. "Except I couldn't remember. What is a resources?"

Owl looked at Pooh sternly. " 'Resources' is plural. Properly you should say, 'What *are*—' "

"Oh. Thank you, Owl," said Pooh. "I didn't know that. What *are* a resources?"

Owl decided to ignore Pooh's inadequate grasp of the basic rules of English grammar and proceeded to the business at hand. "A resource is something that lies ready for use or can be drawn upon for aid. Indisputably, The Stranger meant to explore what resources are and how they can be used to carry out the plans that have been devised to attain the goals that therein have been set."

"I see," said Pooh, although he didn't, really.

"So do I," squeaked Piglet excitedly. "That would be like what happened when we all went on an Expotition to the North Pole and Roo fell into the stream accidentally when he was washing his face and paws."

Piglet shivered at just the thought of it. He didn't much care for washing and agreed with Eeyore that it was just modern behind-the-ears nonsense. Besides being uncomfortable, washing had a tendency to change your color.

"Look at me swimming!" squeaked Roo from the middle of his pool, and was hurried down a waterfall into the next pool.

"Are you all right, Roo dear?" called Kanga anxiously.

"Yes," said Roo. "Look at me sw—" and down he went over the next waterfall into another pool.

Everybody was doing something to help. Piglet, wide awake suddenly, was jumping up and down and making "Oo, I say" noises; Owl was explaining that in a case of Sudden and Temporary Immersion the Important Thing was to keep the Head Above Water; Kanga was jumping along the bank, saying "Are you *sure* you're all right, Roo dear?" to which Roo, from whatever pool he was in at the moment, was answering "Look at me swimming!" Eeyore had turned round and hung his tail over the first pool into which Roo fell, and with his back to the accident was grumbling quietly to himself, and saying, "All this washing; but catch on to my tail, little Roo, and you'll be all right"; and Christopher Robin and Rabbit

came hurrying past Eeyore, and were calling out to the others in front of them.

"All right, Roo, I'm coming," called Christopher Robin.

"Get something across the stream lower down, some of you fellows," called Rabbit.

But Pooh was getting something. Two pools below Roo he was standing with a long pole in his paws, and Kanga came up and took one end of it, and between them they held it across the lower part of the pool; and Roo, still bubbling proudly, "Look at me swimming," drifted up against it, and climbed out.

"So that's an example of a resource," said Piglet. "The pole lay there ready for use and could be drawn upon for aid. Which it was. To rescue Roo."

"Not that it matters," grumbled Eeyore, "but there was another resource there. It's all right not to mention it, but still, it was there and ready to help if needed. If one didn't think it might be needed, one would not have immersed one's tail in the almost freezing water.

It's not as if one enjoys a numbed tail. No feeling in a tail is most uncomfortable. It makes you think you might have lost it, which is worrisome. If you've ever lost a tail"—Eeyore shook his head from side to side—"you'd know that. Not that I suppose many of you have done so."

"I'm sorry, Eeyore," said Piglet. "I was going to mention your tail, but you were too quick for me. Your tail is a splendid resource!"

"I think it is," said Eeyore, looking back to make certain that it was still there. "Although some might not think so."

"I do," said Pooh. "I remember finding yours when it was lost, and at the time I didn't even realize it was a resource as well as a tail, not to speak of a bellpull."

"Most don't," said Eeyore gloomily.

"But now that we know that resources are tails and poles," Pooh continued, "especially poles that are North, and found by Certain Bears"—Pooh tried to look modest, and failed—"it isn't even necessary for The Stranger to tell us about them. If we knew where he was we could tell him that he doesn't have to be 'Backson' because we know about resources."

Just as Pooh said that, The Stranger came into view and joined them.

All the usual Hallos and Greetings were said and Pooh just happened to mention that he hadn't realized that "Backson" was now, because he would have

thought that it was much earlier and The Stranger said that Pooh was right, it was earlier. The Stranger was sorry that "Backson" had been so long ago but there had been an Unavoidable Delay.

The Stranger had taken off his backpack, propped it against the picnic hamper he had put down against the tree trunk, and made himself comfortable. "As I came through the woods, I thought I heard someone saying that they knew about resources. Why don't we start by you telling me what you know about them so that I won't cover the same ground."

"Certainly," said Pooh, wondering if the backpack, in addition to the hamper, might have food in it. "We wouldn't want you to have to go back into the woods when you've just got here."

The Stranger was about to ask why Pooh thought it might be necessary for him to go back into the woods, but decided that it would be better to listen to what they knew about resources.

Pooh proceeded to tell The Stranger how Owl had defined "resources" and how they (really Piglet) had decided what resources were, with the North Pole being mentioned prominently and Eeyore's tail bringing up the rear.

"Tails count too," Eeyore added. "They're not just a Little Bit Extra at the back."

"Of course they do," said The Stranger. "Owl's definition of what a resource is, or what resources are, is exactly correct. You have all done very well in my absence, but I'd like to talk just a little bit more about what resources are, how you decide what resources are needed to carry out your plans, and how the effective use of available resources will allow you to achieve your goals more expeditiously."

They all agreed, although Eeyore grumbled, "So there's more to resources than tails and poles. I might have known."

"The first thing to remember," The Stranger continued, "is that resources can be as varied as the steps in your plan. Resources are not only tails and poles, although in the case you mentioned, Piglet, they were.

"However, let's talk about the more common resources that are usually involved in any project or steps of an action plan for achieving a goal. There are four that are almost always helpful. They are time, money, knowledge, and skills. Proper utilization of those will help you to complete most steps in any plan and most steps will require one or more of these resources."

"I usually have time," said Eeyore. "I suppose one out of four is the best one might do. It's probably better than I expected, now that I think about it."

"You shouldn't feel bad at all," said The Stranger. "Time is probably the most important resource of all, because it is limited. Each one of us has the same amount—twenty-four hours a day. No more, no less.

It's not the amount of time we have that is important, it's how we manage it. How we utilize it to achieve what we want."

"You might know," said Eeyore disgustedly. "It's the only resource I have and it turns out that everyone has the same amount of it. Not at all special that—"

"As a mother," interrupted Kanga, "it seems to me that there is never enough time to do everything that I should do. I'd like to know what I could do to help *that* situation."

"I'd be willing to give up baths and taking my Strengthening Medicine," squeaked Roo. "That might give you more time to do other things."

"I'd be happy to eat any Extract of Malt that Roo doesn't," offered Tigger.

"Now, Roo," said Kanga, "you know that those are both needed if you are to grow up into a strong and handsome kangaroo."

"I thought it was a good idea," said Roo, disappointed.

"So did I," said Tigger, licking his lips.

"It was a good idea in principle," said The Stranger. "Except that you picked the wrong things to eliminate in order to utilize your time more effectively. If you picked things that were not important, your idea would be a good one."

Piglet, who had brightened up at hearing Roo's suggestion about baths, muttered something about not thinking very much of this whole time-utilization idea as a resource.

"What we want to do," said The Stranger, "is to utilize the fixed amount of time that we have wisely, so that we can accomplish our goals. That's a subject we will learn about later. What's more, Kanga, I guarantee, if you use the things we'll talk about, you'll find that you can do everything you have to do and more besides."

"Good," said Kanga, settling herself to listen, although being a mother she was not so certain.

"The next resource we mentioned was money," The Stranger continued. "Much of the time the steps in your Plan that you have developed to achieve your goals or goal will not require money. However, sometimes money can be used to make the completion of the step much easier. Can anybody give me an idea of how this could be?"

"Money is defined as a Medium of Exchange," offered Owl. "Perhaps you could exchange money for something that you didn't have or something that you needed in a larger quantity than you had available. Like time, which you said was limited."

"Very good, Owl!" said The Stranger. "If you had a step in your Plan that required twenty hours of your time to complete and you wanted to get it done more quickly, you could offer to pay someone to help you and then it would be completed in ten hours. What you've done is to exchange money for time."

"That," said Owl sternly, "is just what I said."

"True," said The Stranger. "However, I wanted to emphasize it by repeating it because it's an important lesson when you are thinking about resources. You see, what Owl's example shows us is that in a certain sense money can be the same as time. We say that time equals money, which implies that they are interchangeable. If you require a certain amount of time, you can substitute money and if you need a certain amount of money you can sometimes substitute time. This is often true of other resources as well, so you should be alert to the possibility."

"Like when Owl wanted to move his things to a new house after his old one blew down on a Very Blusterous Day," said Rabbit. "We could have paid a moving company to do it, but instead we all pitched in and did it ourselves."

"Exactly, Rabbit. That's a very good example," The

Stranger complimented. "Just remember 'Money equals Time' and that you can sometimes substitute one resource for another."

"What about the other two," said Pooh. "Knowledge and—ah—Skills. Are they the same as time and money?"

"In the sense that you can use time to gain knowledge. School is an example of that—"

Piglet perked up. That was something that he knew something about.

"—and," The Stranger continued, "if you have money you can hire someone to find the knowledge you need or to tutor you. Most of the time, a good way to get knowledge is to read about what you want to know in a book, or if you have a computer, go on something called the Internet or the World Wide Web—"

Piglet's ears twitched. The thought of one of Rabbit's friends being large enough to weave a spiderweb that size was hard to imagine.

"—or ask someone who knows," continued The Stranger.

"That's what I do," said Pooh. "I usually ask Christopher Robin, or if he's not around I ask Owl or someone else."

Owl had been perched on a branch with his eyes closed. He might have been having Forty Winks, or he might not have been. It was difficult to say because he often perched that way during the day. "The light is too bright," he would say if Pooh or someone else asked him if he were sleeping. This time he must have heard his name because his eyes opened, and he fluffed up his feathers and said, "Who?"

Pooh thought for a moment about who the some-one else might be.

"It depends on what I want to know. If someone is not feeling well, I ask Kanga what should be done. For things about organizing things, Rabbit is usually good. Piglet knows lots about Haycorns and Heffalumps. For thistles, there is no one better than Eeyore."

"Last as usual," said Eeyore. "Still, thistles are an important subject and I've heard Christopher Robin say that you save the best for last. Although he may have been talking about cakes with icing on the top and your name in pink sugar and candles and—"

"A thistle," Owl interrupted, "is the common name of the prickly herbaceous plant of the composite genus *Carduus*," just to show that if Eeyore were in a different part of the Forest there were others who could be relied upon.

"Thank you, Owl," said Pooh. "I didn't really want to know just now, that is."

Eeyore and Owl both "Humphed."

"You have the right idea, Pooh," said The Stranger quickly, so that there wouldn't be an argument as to which one knew the most about thistles. "Asking others is one way to gain knowledge, particularly if you ask those who know about the subject."

Pooh tried to look modest.

"Now we come to the last of the commonly needed resources—Skills," The Stranger continued. "In particular we want to talk about the skills that each individual might have. You see, when you are carrying out a Plan, often some of the steps will require certain skills. To help us in this area, it's a good idea to do a Skills Inventory."

"What is a Skills Inventory?" said Piglet, having raised his hand first. "Also, what is a Skill?"

"That's a good question, Piglet," said The Stranger. "A Skill is something that you do well. Something that you are proficient at accomplishing. A Skills Inventory is a list of all the different things that you know how to do. It might include basic things like telling stories or finding your way in the Forest or more complicated things like programming a computer or writing or—"

"Solving problems!" said Pooh, proud that a Bear of Very Little Brain had become quite a Problem Solver.

"But why do you do it?" asked Roo.

"Because problems are there," said Pooh determinedly.

"No." Roo shook his head. "I mean why do you make up a Skills Inventory?"

"There are several reasons, Roo," said The

Stranger. "Doing a Skills Inventory or reviewing one on a regular basis can help give you confidence in your skills as well as more awareness of them. It can also show you where you might want to improve your skills or learn new ones. Considering your skills as a resource allows you to look at the steps you have listed in a Plan to accomplish a goal and see what skills you can provide and what you might need to find elsewhere."

"But doesn't everyone know what their skills are?" asked Roo.

"Not always," said The Stranger. "Some are too modest about their own skills. Or they tend to compartmentalize them. That is, they don't realize that a skill like keeping financial records for their church is applicable to doing the same for a small business. Skills are transferable and often can be used in other ways and other conditions."

Pooh had been trying hard to listen, but had got confused right in the middle of what The Stranger was saying.

"I think I'm confused," he said.

The Stranger leaned his head back, looking up at the branches of the tree under which they were sitting.

After a while he nodded. "I think this might be easier to understand if we use an example, and I think I've thought of the perfect one."

The Stranger looked around at the others. "How many

of you know anything about building a tree swing?"

They all looked slowly at each other to see who might know, but no one raised his hand or said anything.

"All right," said The Stranger, "let me ask again, but this time I'll express it a little differently. How many here know anything about climbing trees, walking on branches, finding things, tying knots, or trying new things?"

"Tiggers are the best at all those things," said Tigger. "Except climbing down trees."

"I'm good at climbing," said Roo. "Up. If Tigger helps."

"I can tie knots," said Piglet proudly. "Christopher Robin showed me how."

"And I'm very good at trying new things," said Pooh. "Like rhymes and new jars of honey."

"Very good," said The Stranger. "Those are skills

that are used in building a tree swing. Now Roo, why didn't you answer the first time when I asked if you knew how to build tree swings?"

"I . . . I . . . suppose I didn't realize," said Roo slowly, "that part of building a tree swing was climbing."

"Excellent," said The Stranger. "That's the point I was trying to make. One of the best reasons to do a Skills Inventory is to find out what skills are available to be called upon. An important point to remember in listing our skills is to look at them in a way that characterizes the essence of the skill and not the specific setting it may have been used in in the past. So we'd list Roo's skill as 'climbing,' not as 'climbing trees' or 'climbing ladders.' "

"Is it the same thing for tying knots?" squeaked Piglet.

"What do you mean?" asked The Stranger.

"Well," said Piglet, "when Christopher Robin taught me how it was with his shoes, and while that is very useful, if you're the kind who wears shoes, that is, it didn't seem like the kind of thing that would be useful for something else, unless you had another pair of shoes."

"And that's exactly the point! Thank you, Piglet!" said The Stranger, while Piglet took a slight bow and beamed with pride. "We must remember to examine our skills openly and without modesty to see what their potential is for helping us with the task we are working on."

The Stranger paused for a minute while he was thinking. "I think it will be best if we actually do a Skills Inventory. Piglet, may we use you as our example?"

Piglet blushed, although nobody could tell since it was quite some time since his bath at Kanga's. "Yes," he said.

"All right," said The Stranger. "What skills do you have other than tying knots?"

"Well . . . er . . . uh," stammered Piglet. "I can't think of anything. You don't suppose it's because I don't really have any skills, do you?"

"Not at all. Everyone has skills, but if you haven't done this before, it might seem a bit difficult the first time.

"So, Piglet," said The Stranger, "to begin your Skills Inventory we will make a list of all the things that you are good at or have experience at. And I'd like the rest of you to help Piglet by mentioning skills you think he has."

"Trapping Heffalumps," said Pooh. "Piglet is very good at trapping Heffalumps."

Piglet swallowed hard, remembering how frightened he had been and hoping that just because you were good at something didn't mean that you actually had to do it.

"Impersonating small animals," added Roo. "Remember when you took my place?"

"And being small and nimble, tied to a string and lifted up to the letter box," said Pooh.

"And writing messages to be rescued," added Piglet himself, very proud of his thoughtfulness during that particular adventure.

"And b—" Pooh almost started to say "building Eeyore a house," but not being certain if Eeyore knew they had built it, he quickly changed it to "—being generous, when Owl needed a house."

"Those are very fine skills," said The Stranger. "Look."

They all gathered around and looked at the ground where The Stranger had smoothed a space, taken a stick, and printed:

PIGLET'S SKILLS INVENTORY

Hunting and trapping

Acting

Climbing

Writing

Donating and Giving

"That's an excellent start, Piglet!" said The Stranger. "I'll make a copy of it so that you can add to it when you learn new skills."

So The Stranger worked with them and soon each had a list. Pooh's list looked something like this:

POOH'S SKILLS INVENTORY

Imitating Clouds

Eating Honey

Rescuing (Piglets and Roos, mostly)

Hooshing

Testing Honey (to make sure it is still good)

Playing Poohsticks

Humming Hums (and making them up)

Trying New Things (Like honey and Problem Solving)

Problem Solving

Pooh scratched his head. "Now that we have our lists," he said, "how do we use them? It's the 'Hows' that give me trouble."

"That's a good point, Pooh," said The Stranger. "If we just stopped after making up the list it wouldn't help very much. Once we have our list—or several lists if we are working with others—we review them when we have something we want done, a new job or position to fill, or a project to do. Many managers will keep lists for each of the people they supervise so they can do just that when the need arises."

"Like a tree swing to build!" said Roo excitedly.

"Exactly," said The Stranger. "We use the lists of skills to remind us of all the different things that each of us does, and to assign parts of the new projects to be done."

The Stranger had been looking at each of the lists as he talked. He stopped in front of Tigger's, which was now very hard to read since he had been bouncing all over it since Piglet had finished helping him write it down. It listed every skill that was on everyone else's list, including "Eating Honey."

"Tigger," said The Stranger, "do Tiggers really like eating honey?"

"Oh, yes," said Tigger. "Eating honey is what Tiggers do best."

"Are you sure?" asked The Stranger. "I seem to remember something else."

"That's right," said Pooh. "There's even a poem about it." And he began to recite.

> What shall we do about poor little Tigger?
> If he never eats nothing he'll never get bigger.
> He doesn't like honey and haycorns and thistles
> Because of the taste and because of the bristles.
> And all the good things which an animal likes
> Have the wrong sort of swallow or too many spikes.

"We should remember that it is important to be realistic when listing your skills," said The Stranger. "Be certain that you only list those that you honestly feel capable of carrying out and performing."

Tigger looked very unbouncy.

"I'm afraid that I still don't understand how to use the Skills Inventory," said Pooh.

"Perhaps if we build a tree swing, that will be better than my explaining," said The Stranger. "Will you all help?"

"Oh, yes!" they all cried.

"Good. To build a swing, we need to know what resources are needed, both in the way of materials and skills."

"That's another thing I don't understand," said Pooh. "How do you decide how much in the way of resources you will need?"

"You estimate what will be needed. An estimate is

a sort of a guess. If you've done something like it before, you can come pretty close. If you are wrong, you just have to change your estimate and get more or fewer resources as you do the job."

"Oh," said Pooh. "I can guess pretty well."

"I'd guess we'd get the swing made and then it would rain," said Eeyore.

"What resources do we need?" asked Piglet.

"I've built swings before," said The Stranger, "so I can make a pretty good estimate. We will need to select a tree, then find about thirty feet of strong rope and a board about eight inches wide, three-quarters of an inch thick, and two feet or so long. We need to find the best strong branch to tie the swing to, tie the rope to the branch and tie it to the board, and then we should test it out to make certain it's safe."

"That sounds like an awful lot of work," said Pooh, looking about for a smackerel in case it took a long time to build the swing.

"I would estimate that it won't take long at all with the skills we have here. I'd say that before it's time for tea we will have it up. Then we can celebrate by having a little something."

Good! thought Pooh. Now I can see how you estimate what resources are needed. You need enough to finish in time for tea and a smackerel. He thought for a moment. And you need the resources for the tea and the smackerel.

Before having everyone decide whose skills were best suited to carry out parts of the project, The Stranger changed Tigger's list to reflect a more realistic view of his particular skills ("Bouncing" and "Climbing Up, but not Down" were left on), and then everyone looked at the lists and discussed who would be best. The Stranger explained that this was something that one individual could do by himself but if there was a group involved it was usually better if the members of the group were involved. In this case it also gave everyone practice in working with the Skills Inventory.

After considerable discussion, Piglet was assigned the task of finding the rope and a board because of his skills in hunting. (Piglet was greatly relieved that he hadn't been assigned to trap a Heffalump.) He meandered off, humming to himself.

Tigger and Roo were to select the right tree and branch because they could cover a lot of ground in a hurry with Roo riding on Tigger's back.

The Stranger's skills included knot tying on swings, so he was given that job and was instructed to use special knots that wouldn't hurt the tree and wouldn't come undone either.

Once the tree and the branch were selected, Eeyore was to make certain that the area directly under the swing and for a reasonable distance around it (The Stranger estimated ten feet) was free of thistles and gorse bushes and other Prickly Things.

Owl was to provide messenger service, if needed, which it wasn't, and also to be a lookout for individuals returning with resources (mostly Piglet) in case they needed help.

Pooh, being of about the right degree of stoutness, and because of his skill in trying new things, was given the job of being the tester, once the swing was put up.

Kanga was the overall supervisor, standby nurse, and first-aid individual, more than qualified by being the only mother present.

Faster than anyone would have thought, the tree swing came together. The Stranger pulled on his knots and, satisfied that they would hold, stood back, motioning to Pooh that it was time for him to do the testing.

They all watched and held their breath as Pooh got on the swing and began to swing back and forth, higher and higher, until it seemed he would almost touch the clouds.

"What if it doesn't hold?" said Piglet, convinced that at any moment the rope would break and Pooh would be thrown clear out of the Forest. But it did hold.

After Pooh had tested it thoroughly, the others each had a turn, and even The Stranger got on and whooshed back and forth.

The Stranger, who was swinging almost as high as Pooh had, let go of the ropes when the swing reached the top of its travel, and was launched off the seat. He kept on going and going, tracing an arc through the air. Piglet was the first to see where The Stranger would land, and shouted, "Oh, no! Oh, no! Stop!"

As much as Piglet shouted, The Stranger kept going, clear over a row of bushes and into a patch of burly thistles almost twenty feet from the swing!

"*Owowwwww!*" cried The Stranger, getting up very, very gingerly.

"I know how you feel," said Pooh, trying to be comforting. "That's happened to me. Falling on a thistle, that is."

The others, including Kanga ready to carry out her assigned nursing and first-aid duties, rushed to where The Stranger had landed.

Fortunately, except for his dignity and a few stickers and spikes in various parts, The Stranger was unhurt. "I was trying to jump and land on my feet," he explained.

"So I guess that 'Jumping and Landing' can't be listed on your Skills Inventory," said Roo.

The Stranger grinned. "No, and I guess I better remove 'Estimating' from it also. I thought ten feet free of thistles would be enough."

Eeyore looked at where The Stranger had landed and sadly shook his head. "You didn't do the thistles any good," he said. "I've said again and again that sitting on them doesn't do them any good. Takes all the

life out of them. I suppose that I also should have reminded certain individuals"—Eeyore looked sternly at The Stranger—"that jumping on them from a great height is even worse. Particularly when the individual thrashes around after landing. One tries to cover everything, but it is difficult."

"I'm sorry, Eeyore," said The Stranger, picking thistles out of sensitive parts. "You have no idea how sorry. In any event, have we learned some things about resources, and using a Skills Inventory to help us on completing a project or steps in any Plan?"

"Yes," they all chorused, except for Pooh, who looked at the hamper and said, "And we finished just in time for tea and smackerels. Your estimate there was very good."

"You're right, Pooh Bear. Since I have to leave right after tea and smackerels, why don't I summarize what we've talked about today, while you get the food out?"

Pooh agreed enthusiastically and all the others sat down in a circle at the base of the tree near the slowly moving swing propelled gently back and forth by a soft breeze whispering through the Forest.

"Today," The Stranger began, "we learned about

the various kinds of resources that we might need to carry out Plans, which will lead us to our goal of being successful (however each of us defines that goal). We learned about Money and Time and how they can be interchangeable. We also talked about the need for Knowledge and how we can often find it by asking individuals who know, or consulting a library or even new technology like the Internet or the World Wide Web. We learned how to assess the full range of capabilities for an individual or a group by carrying out a Skills Inventory."

The Stranger paused to take a bite of a little cake with pink sugar icing. "Let's see. Did I forget anything else that we learned how to do?"

"Build a swing," squeaked Roo.

"Not to fall on a thistle from a great height," added Eeyore. "Not to thrash about on Landing, and to work on the skill of Estimating."

"Perfect, Eeyore," said The Stranger, standing up and picking up his backpack and the hamper that Pooh had ever so helpfully emptied. "That's just what we'll talk about tomorrow. We'll learn how to enhance, improve, and strengthen our skills and abilities and how and when to acquire new ones."

The Stranger left the circle. As he came to the edge of the woods he turned and waved. "Thanks for all your help, and we'll meet at the Sandy Pit at ten o'clock for Elevenses tomorrow."

As The Stranger disappeared into the trees, Pooh said, "At least he didn't say 'Back soon' and he did mention 'Elevenses,' which is a promising thing for one to say."

"Wheeeee!" yelled Roo, swinging high in the sky.

VI

In which A Horrible Heffalump May
Be Trapped in the Sandy Pit,
Enhancing Skills and Abilities
Is Discussed, and The Stranger
Gets a Birdie

Pooh and Piglet were late. At least they thought they were. They weren't quite sure, as they didn't remember if they had told The Stranger that they would meet him at a quarter *before* ten or a quarter *after* ten at the Sandy Pit.

"I think we're late, Pooh," said Piglet.

"We're not late until we get there and things have already started," replied Pooh.

Pooh did not like to hurry. When you hurried, you didn't get a chance to see all the things in the Hundred Acre Wood that were so interesting when you weren't in a hurry. And you certainly didn't get a chance to practice any of your hums, or even make up new ones. He tried to make up a hum about hurrying, but it was no use, what with Piglet saying "Oh, we have to go faster!" and "We're almost there!" and such all the time.

Piglet scurried ahead and ran smack into something large and gray and stopped in front of the Sandy Pit.

Pooh ran right into Piglet, and all of them—Pooh, Piglet, and the gray thing—went down in a heap.

"I should have known," said the gray thing. "Just my luck to be standing right where the train was going to come through."

"Eeyore!" cried Piglet.

"Eeyore!" cried Pooh, and they got up and began to dust themselves off.

"Well, of course it's me. Who else would it be? And besides . . ." Eeyore's voice trailed off as they all noticed at the same time a strange commotion in the Sandy Pit.

First there was a thump. Then a spray of sand flew over the small hillock that obscured most of the Pit from their view. Then there was a loud groaning, moaning kind of sound.

Thump! Another rain of sand. "Ooooohh!"

After about ten seconds, thump! Another rain of sand. "Ooooohh!"

"What do you think it could be?" whispered Piglet.

"I don't know," said Pooh.

Thump! Another rain of sand. "Ooooohh!"

"Probably a small earthquake," said Eeyore.

"I hope it isn't a Heffalump," said Piglet, and he

swallowed hard trying to remember just how it was you were supposed to say "Aha" when they appeared, so as to let them know you really weren't afraid.

"If it *is* a Heffalump," said Pooh, "I think he may be trapped."

"And hurt too!" squeaked Piglet. "And a trapped and injured Heffalump is a most dangerous thing. Why, it's probably so desperate it wouldn't even hear one say 'Aha' and react the way it normally would."

"Perhaps we should go and see," said Pooh.

Thump! Another rain of sand. "Ooooohh!"

"I don't think so, Pooh," said Piglet. "What if it's not completely trapped? What if it's only somewhat trapped? Seeing us, it might break free and . . ." At this point Piglet's imagination overtook him and it was all he could do to just stand there shivering.

"If only Owl were here," said Pooh.

"Did I hear my name?" asked Owl, who just at that moment flew up next to them.

"Owl!" cried Pooh. "I'm so glad you're here. We need your help."

"Well, I was just circumnavigating this copse of conifers, when I became aware of a loud and distracting commotion over here. . . ."

Thump! Another rain of sand. "Ooooohh!"

"Owl," said Pooh, "we think that a Heffalump has become trapped in the Sandy Pit, and as we don't want to go look—"

"For fear that he might break free," added Piglet.

"—I thought you might be able to fly over and see just how big the Heffalump is and whether or not he is Completely Trapped or Just Somewhat Trapped."

"I shall be happy to," said Owl. And with a swish of his wings, off he went high up over the small hillock, circling twice and then returning to where the three of them were standing.

Owl was huffing and puffing when he set down. "Huff . . . not what you thought . . . huff, huff . . . not Heffalump . . . huff, huff . . . Stranger . . . huff, huff . . . not alone . . ." was all he could say.

"OOOOhhh!" cried Piglet. "It's not a Heffalump. It's stranger than a Heffalump. It must be a Backson! A Spotted Herbaceous Backson! And he's not alone!" At this point Piglet began running back and forth, trying to decide which direction would afford him the best chance of escape.

"I should have known,"
said Eeyore, accepting his fate
calmly. "It is the season for
them, you know."

"Wait!" said Pooh. "Owl's
trying to say something else!"

Thump! Another rain of
sand. "Ooooohh!"

"What I said, huff, huff,"
said Owl, "is that it's not a Heffalump, huff, huff, it is
The Stranger, huff, huff, and he is not alone, huff, huff.
Roo is with him."

"And is it safe?" asked Piglet.

"Perfectly," said Owl.

And with that, Pooh, Piglet, Eeyore, and Owl
walked around the side of the Sandy Pit and looked
into it. There was The Stranger, a long metal stick in
his hands, with Roo standing behind him. It appeared
he was trying to hit a small round white rock with the
stick. Only he missed and a spray of sand went up over
the hill.

Thump! Another rain of sand. "Ooooohh!"

It seemed The Stranger was the one who was moaning too.

"Hallo!" shouted Pooh.

"Ah! Hallo!" said The Stranger. "There you are.
I've been waiting for you."

"Hi, Pooh! Hi, Piglet! Hi, Eeyore!" called Roo.

"What are you doing?" asked Pooh.

"We thought you were a Heffalump," said Piglet. "A Somewhat Trapped and Dangerous Heffalump."

"Today we are going to talk about acquiring and maintaining new skills," said The Stranger, "so I thought I would show you the importance of practice."

"But what is it you are practicing?" asked Pooh.

"You remember that when we started our conversations, we talked about considering your resources. One resource we discussed was the skills you currently have. While this is very useful, you may have set a goal that requires skills that you *don't* have. In that case, it is a skill you must acquire to be able to reach your goal." At this point The Stranger walked back and stood over the small white rock, and suddenly raised the metal stick he was holding back over his shoulder and swung down hard.

Thump! Another rain of sand. "Ooooohh!" said The Stranger.

"So you see," said The Stranger, "some skills require a great deal of practice if one is to become adept."

"What's a dept?" asked Piglet.

"But what is it you are practicing?" asked Pooh again.

"It is quite obvious," said Owl, "that he is repetitively attempting to strike the white spheroid in such a way as to remove it from the Sandy Pit, obviously as part of his practicing a derivation of the ancient Roman game, paganica. That is to say, he is playing golf."

"Gowf?" said Piglet.

"Golf," said Eeyore. "My kind of game. Whacking a very small ball with a stick around the countryside until it goes in a hole and you can't see it any longer."

"Yes," said The Stranger. "Golf is a game where you hit a small ball with a club, like this one," he said, holding up the metal stick, "from a starting point called a tee, toward a target, a small hole with a flag in it. If you are good, you hit birdies and eagles."

"I don't think," said Pooh, "that this sounds like my kind of game. Hurting birds."

"No, no, no," said The Stranger, laughing, "you've misunderstood. A birdie is just a nickname for when you take fewer strokes to complete a hole than a practiced player would on the same hole. . . ." The Stranger noticed the glazed expression on Pooh's face, and Piglet's too. "Well, that's a long story. Let's talk some more about Strengthening Abilities.

"Some skills," The Stranger continued, "require practice so they can be maintained or improved. I brought along my golf club—"

"You don't really think he hits birds with it, do you?" Piglet asked Pooh in a quiet voice.

"—to be able to show you how I was trying to improve my golf game. Particularly my play out of the

sand. By coming out here to the Sandy Pit and practicing this shot over and over again, I hope to become
better so that when I play, I can play better."

"Looks like you still need to practice," said Eeyore,
gazing over at where the small white golf ball was half-
buried in the sand.

"And one of the ways to do this," said The
Stranger, "is to make sure to build in your practice of
skills when you create your Plan. If there is a new skill
that you want to acquire, include your practice in your
Plan. In this way you are recognizing that acquiring
that skill will take some time, and that you are doing
exactly what you should be doing, practicing, to gain
that skill."

"Like humming," said Pooh. "A new hum doesn't
always come out just the way it should. But after a
couple of tries, it seems to decide what it's going to be
like, and then it does. Come out right, that is."

"That's right, Pooh," said The Stranger. "In that
case, you are practicing your hums so that they come
out better. Another important part of acquiring a new

skill or maintaining an existing one is to practice with purpose. Practicing with purpose means that each time you perform the activity, you do it with the intent of improving, either by working on one specific part of the overall skill, or by trying to improve on one part of the ability. Practicing without a specific purpose is not bad, but it is not as effective as setting small improvements and targets for yourself in your practice session. In this way, each time you practice, you are able to make progress that brings you closer to mastering this skill that is needed to achieve your goal."

"How often should you practice?" asked Roo.

"As often as you can," said The Stranger. "Because if you have to acquire a skill to be able to accomplish your goal, the more rapidly you acquire that skill, whether it be learning a language, finding out how to do accounting, or hitting a golf ball, the sooner you can put that skill to use to accomplish your goal. Another important point about skills is that you may find that you need to continue to revisit them regularly and practice a skill or ability to be able to maintain your performance at the desired level. And here again, it is important to remember to include in your Plan the time necessary to practice those necessary skills."

"I think I need to revisit my larder," said Pooh, who was quite suddenly hungry, as though he had missed Elevenses altogether.

"For instance," said The Stranger, "I remember the time that you, Piglet, and Pooh had fallen into a pit while you were searching for Small. And you were worried that there might be a Heffalump in the Pit with you. And so you began to practice what you might do if you were to come upon a Heffalump."

"What happens when the Heffalump comes?" asked Piglet tremblingly, when he had heard the news.

"Perhaps he won't notice *you*, Piglet," said Pooh encouragingly, "because you're a Very Small Animal."

"But he'll notice *you*, Pooh."

"He'll notice *me*, and I shall notice *him*," said Pooh, thinking it out. "We'll notice each other for a long time, and then he'll say: 'Ho-*ho*!' "

Piglet shivered a little at the thought of that "Ho-*ho*!" and his ears began to twitch.

"W-what will *you* say?" he asked.

Pooh tried to think of something he would say, but the more he thought, the more he felt that there *is* no real answer to "Ho-*ho*!" said by a Heffalump in the sort of voice this Heffalump was going to say it in.

"I shan't say anything," said Pooh at last. "I shall just hum to myself, as if I was waiting for something."

"Then perhaps he'll say, 'Ho-*ho*!' again?" suggested Piglet anxiously.

"He will," said Pooh.

Piglet's ears twitched so quickly that he had to lean them against the side of the Trap to keep them quiet.

"He will say it again," said Pooh, "and I shall go on humming. And that will Upset him. Because when you say 'Ho-*ho*' twice, in a gloating sort of way, and the other person only hums, you suddenly find, just as you begin to say it the third time—that—well, you find—"

"What?"

"That it isn't," said Pooh.

"Isn't what?"

Pooh knew what he meant, but, being a Bear of Very Little Brain, couldn't think of the words.

"Well, it just isn't," he said again.

"You mean it isn't ho-*ho*-ish any more?" said Piglet hopefully.

Pooh looked at him admiringly and said that that was what he meant—if you went on humming all the time, because you couldn't go on saying "Ho-*ho*!" for ever.

"But he'll say something else," said Piglet.

"That's just it. He'll say: 'What's all this?' And then *I* shall say—and this is a very good idea, Piglet, which I've just thought of—I shall say: 'It's a trap for a Heffalump which I've made, and I'm waiting for the Heffalump to fall in.' And I shall go on humming. That will Unsettle him."

"Pooh!" cried Piglet, and now it was *his* turn to be the admiring one. "You've saved us!"

"Have I?" said Pooh, not feeling quite sure.

But Piglet was quite sure; and his mind ran on, and he saw Pooh and the Heffalump talking to each other, and he thought suddenly, and a little sadly, that it *would* have been rather nice if it had been Piglet and the Heffalump talking so grandly to each other and not Pooh, much as he loved Pooh; because he really had more brain than Pooh, and the conversation would go better if he and not Pooh were doing one side of it, and it would be comforting afterwards in the evenings to look back on the day when he answered a Heffalump back as bravely as if the Heffalump wasn't there. It seemed so easy now. He knew just what he would say.

"That's very good, Piglet," said The Stranger.

"Talking to a Horrible Heffalump?" asked Piglet.

"No. It is very good that you were *pretending* to be talking to a Horrible Heffalump. Role-playing is an excellent exercise for practicing certain things," said The Stranger, patting Piglet on the back.

"And much safer than real-playing," said Piglet proudly.

"Hooray, Piglet!" shouted Roo.

HEFFALUMP (*gloatingly*): "Ho-*ho!*"

PIGLET (*carelessly*): "Tra-la-la, tra-la-la."

HEFFALUMP (*surprised, and not quite so sure of himself*): "Ho-*ho!*"

PIGLET (*more carelessly still*): "Tiddle-um-tum, tiddle-um-tum."

HEFFALUMP (*beginning to say Ho-ho and turning it awkwardly into a cough*): "H'r'm! What's all this?"

PIGLET (*surprised*): "Hullo! This is a trap I've made, and I'm waiting for a Heffalump to fall into it."

HEFFALUMP (*greatly disappointed*): "Oh!" (*after a long silence*): "Are you sure?"

PIGLET: "Yes."

HEFFALUMP: "Oh!" (*nervously*): "I—I thought it was a trap I'd made to catch Piglets."

PIGLET (*surprised*): "Oh, no!"

HEFFALUMP: "Oh!" (*apologetically*): "I—I must have got it wrong, then."

PIGLET: "I'm afraid so." (*politely*): "I'm sorry." (*He goes on humming.*)

HEFFALUMP: "Well—well—I—well. I suppose I'd better be getting back?"

PIGLET (*looking up carelessly*): "Must you? Well, if you see Christopher Robin anywhere, you might tell him I want him."

HEFFALUMP (*eager to please*): "Certainly! Certainly!" (*He hurries off.*)

POOH (*who wasn't going to be there, but we find we can't do without him*): "Oh, Piglet, how brave and clever you are!"

PIGLET (*modestly*): "Not at all, Pooh." (*And then, when Christopher Robin comes, Pooh can tell him all about it.*)

"So by practicing what to do," said The Stranger, "you were prepared for when a Heffalump showed up."

"But no Heffalump *did* show up," said Piglet.

"Yes," said Pooh, "but you were Prepared."

"That's right," said The Stranger. "And should you ever need that skill again, it will be much easier for you to get it."

"I suppose so," said Piglet hesitatingly, remembering how difficult it had been to remember, when he thought The Stranger was a Heffalump. "But I think that I should practice regularly."

"Now, when we want to acquire new skills," said The Stranger, "we first want to identify what those skills and abilities are. This is usually done after the goal has been set, and we are creating a Plan to achieve it. We come across a step in the Plan where a particular skill or ability would make achieving the goal easier. One of *my* goals is to exercise regularly and I play golf as a way of doing that. And one of my desires is to play golf better than I do now. So the skills and abilities that are important to me are to learn how to hit the different shots in golf well, so that I can play better."

"So that is why you are practicing?" asked Roo.

"Yes. But that is not all," said The Stranger. "Once you have decided what skills you want to acquire, it is useful to research what resources are available. Remember our talk about resources? Here we will be searching out information and instruction that will help us to acquire our desired skill as rapidly and easily as possible. For instance, we might go to a library or a bookshop, as there are hundreds of instructional books on golf. Or we might consider instruction at a school with others, or personally seek out an individual who has those skills who might be willing to assist us in learning them. Whether we get our help from the Internet, or from a book, or from a friend, the intent is to research and make use of the different resources available to learn the skill we are interested in acquiring."

"What's an Internet?" asked Pooh.

"Remember, Pooh?" Piglet whispered. "It's one of those giant spiderwebby things he was talking about before."

"It is a multinoded, asynchronous informational network that provides access to user knowledge from other participants," said Owl.

"It's the Information Highway, Pooh," said The Stranger.

"Is that like the M1?" said Piglet, who didn't really know what the M1 was, but had heard that it was a highway.

"Sort of," said The Stranger, "but then that is a completely different story. When we are attempting to learn a new skill, it is important to remember that many skills take a long time to acquire, and that we should be realistic about how long it may take and patient about our progress. And like we do with Plans, it is often helpful to reward yourself when milestones are achieved, or when your practicing is showing progress."

"If you were Very Patient and sat quietly," said Pooh, "all during a talk, and when the talk was over, and you truly felt you had learned something, then might you be able to reward yourself and, say . . . have lunch?"

"Well, that's an excellent idea, Pooh," said The Stranger. "And if you look over by that tree, you will find that I have brought a basket with something for all of us."

"You may all have lunch," said Owl, "but as I was up late last night catching up on my reading—I'm a bit of a night person you know—I think I shall go and take a nap in those trees over there." And off he flew, settling on a branch in one of the trees of the Forest that bordered the open space near the Sandy Pit.

The Stranger retrieved his basket, and everyone

helped spread out the blanket he had brought and pass out the watercress sandwiches and other treats. After they had all eaten their fill, they sat on the blanket and listened to The Stranger.

"Today we talked about how you may need to learn new skills or improve existing skills to be able to accomplish some of your goals. We talked about how some skills require practice to maintain competence or to improve and that this practice should be built into your Plan and schedules. And when you do practice your skills, it is helpful to Practice with Purpose."

"Did he say practice with porpoises?" Piglet asked Pooh.

"I think so," said Pooh sleepily, as he was barely listening himself after the large lunch.

"Just my luck," said Eeyore, "there probably isn't a dolphin in the Forest."

"To maintain your skills," continued The Stranger, "it is helpful to revisit them regularly."

"In case you should meet a Heffalump," said Piglet.

"And in the case of a new skill," said The Stranger, "once we identify the skill that we need, we research the different resources available and use those resources to help us acquire the skill. By setting a realistic regimen and including it in our Plan, and by patiently practicing and learning the new skill, as well as rewarding ourselves for achievements along the way, we will be able to learn the desired skill, and then use that skill to Achieve our Goals."

"Hooray!" said Roo, having got caught up and excited by The Stranger's speech.

"Thank you, Roo," said The Stranger. "So let us see if my practice has paid off." The Stranger got up, picked up his golf club, and walked over to where the ball lay in the sand. "Let's see," he said to himself. "Take an open stance, with the ball forward in the stance . . . the club face open, . . . don't ground the club . . ."

The animals all turned to watch, as they knew that something important was about to happen.

". . . select a position to aim the club at about two inches behind the ball . . ." And with that, The Stranger drew the club back over his shoulder and swung hard at the ball.

There was a loud thump!

And, as before, there was a spray of sand sent into the air.

But this time, there was no moan, as The Stranger had launched the ball into the air. They all watched as the ball sailed up out of the Sandy Pit and lazily arced toward the trees.

"Look out!" cried Roo, who was the first to realize that the ball was headed right to where Owl was perched on a branch taking his nap.

"Fore!" shouted The Stranger.

The ball struck Owl lightly on the head, and, as he was quite asleep, knocked him off the branch. Luckily, he awoke part of the way through his fall and was able to flap his wings enough so that when he hit the ground underneath the tree, it wasn't with too much force.

"I think," said Eeyore, "that's what you would call an Owl-in-one."

"And a birdie too," said Piglet.

They all rushed over to Owl to make sure he was all right. They picked him up and brushed him off, and checked all of his feathers. They decided that he might have strained his Necessary Dorsal Muscles, but that he would be fine. But they also decided that The Stranger shouldn't play any more golf in the Forest until he had practiced a bit more, and with a little different purpose.

The Stranger apologized again, and said that he would be going, that he had quite a lot to do, but that the next time they got together they would talk about the last step in the Success procedure, which was Spending Time Wisely.

The Stranger apologized once more to Owl, who said that he was fine and not to worry, and then he said good-bye and walked off toward the village.

"You don't think this golf will catch on, do you," asked Piglet.

"Not a chance," said Eeyore. "It's too depressing."

"Well," said Owl, "it is about time for Tea, so I am going home. Would any of you like to join me?"

"Oh yes, please," said Piglet, and Pooh nodded too. "Perhaps we can *practice* having tea, with some cakes and honey."

"I shall practice with *purpose*," said Pooh.

VII

In which No One Meets at the Bee Tree to Talk About Spending Time Wisely, and Rabbit Has Another Busy Day

The Stranger arrived at the Bee Tree at the appointed time. It was a beautiful morning and The Stranger had enjoyed the fresh smells of the Forest during his walk to meet his friends this morning.

He was not particularly surprised when he arrived to find that no one was there. Since it was such a nice morning, he was sure they had become distracted by one thing or another and would soon come by.

The Stranger was right, and he was also wrong.

It was quite a while later, and still no one had arrived to meet The Stranger, as they had agreed, to talk about Spending Time Wisely and how it was another important part of being Successful. It was only then that The Stranger heard a far-off kind of humming noise coming from the direction of the Hundred Acre Wood.

The Stranger couldn't quite make out *what* it was that was being hummed, but he was certain he knew *who* was doing the humming.

"Pooh!" said The Stranger when Pooh finally came into sight. "You're here!"

"Am I?" said Pooh, walking up to where The Stranger was and sitting down on a rock.

"What I meant was," said The Stranger, "you are *finally* here. You do remember that we were supposed to meet here this morning and talk about Spending Time Wisely?"

"Oh, yes," said Pooh, but sounding as if he were not too sure at all. "I'm sorry I was late, but I was . . ."

"Distracted?" offered The Stranger.

"Yes. That's it. Detractored," said Pooh. "It being such a wonderful day and all that."

"Well, where do you think everyone else is?" asked The Stranger. "You did tell everyone else about our meeting, didn't you?"

"I hope so. I mean, I think so. I mean . . . let me think." And so Pooh sat and thought. It was hard work to think this morning, what with his hum that he had been humming continually coming back into his head while he was trying to remember if he had asked everyone to remember to meet The Stranger at a meeting that he didn't remember. But then he remembered.

"I have it!" said Pooh. "I remember asking Rabbit to make sure to ask everyone to meet here. He was just

on his way to Owl's house, I think, and he said he was going to see Piglet before he went over to Kanga's house, where Tigger and Roo would be. So I asked him to tell everyone. Was that all right?"

"Certainly, Pooh," said The Stranger. "That is fine. That is a good example of the delegation we learned about when we were talking about Management. But it's a good idea too, to follow up and see that what you've delegated is being done."

"You don't think anything has happened?" asked Pooh, suddenly very worried.

"I think *something* has happened," said The Stranger.

They decided that the best thing to do would be to go to Rabbit's house to see what it was that had happened. On the way they ran into Piglet, who said no, he hadn't seen Rabbit in a couple of days, and that *he* hadn't been told about the meeting and because of that was out gathering haycorns instead of doing whatever it was that he was supposed to have been doing otherwise. He put the few haycorns that he had found in a small neat pile by the base of a tree where he would be able to find them again, and joined Pooh and The Stranger on their way to Rabbit's house. They passed by the Sandy Pit and found Tigger and Roo cavorting in the sand. They, too, had not heard from Rabbit and didn't know about the Meeting. They all joined together and walked on toward Rabbit's house.

When they arrived at Rabbit's house they were surprised to see a great number of Rabbit's friends-and-relations sitting in the grass scattered around in front of the door to his house. Rabbit was racing back and forth from one group to another, and it looked as if he was getting tea for everyone, as there were brightly colored cloths spread out on the ground at each group, and Rabbit was carrying a plate with small watercress sandwiches and a pot of tea around to each of the groups in turn. And sitting among them was Eeyore.

"I couldn't help myself," said Eeyore gloomily. "When Henry Rush came by my house—he's one of the Beetle family, you know—and said there was to be a Tea and Rabbit was giving it, I could hardly refuse."

"Hallo, Rabbit!" said Pooh, trying to get his attention and hoping there were enough watercress sandwiches to go around.

"Not now, Pooh!" said Rabbit as he scurried past.

"Can't you see I'm busy? I'll be with you in a minute, or perhaps I can talk to you later. Yes, that's it. I shall make sure to come to your house later. Thank you so much for coming. Bye now." And off he went from one group to the other.

"But Rabbit!" said Pooh, watching the sandwiches receding. "You're late! You were supposed to meet us."

"I know I'm late," said Rabbit, giving up with an exasperated sigh and coming back to talk with Pooh and the others. "And I'm much too busy to chat just now."

"But don't you remember that you were supposed to meet with The Stranger this morning?"

"Now that you mention it . . . no. But then when you're as busy as I am, it's not surprising. Never enough time, you know. Must get back to my Tea."

"And don't you remember as well," said Pooh, "that you were going to ask all the others to come and meet The Stranger too?"

"If that's what I said," said Rabbit, "then that is what I must have done."

"But you didn't ask me!" squeaked Piglet.

"Or me!" said Tigger.

"Me too!" said Roo.

"Well," said Rabbit, "then I must have forgotten. You truly cannot expect me to do everything, you know. And I really can't do anything about it right now, what with all this company and everything. . . ."

"Perhaps we can help," said The Stranger. "We were just about to sit down and talk about the importance of Spending Time Wisely. And it seems that you, too, could benefit. It is such an important part of being Successful, and I know that you would thank me for it later."

"Oh, couldn't possibly!" said Rabbit. "I've got all this company, and then I have to clean up, and then I was going to go over to Owl's house, and then . . . I've just got too much to do!"

"But this talk will help you to organize your time more effectively," said The Stranger. "To become better at doing those things that are most important to get done."

"Not possible," said Rabbit. "I'm much too busy to become more effective."

"That's exactly why," said The Stranger. "Tigger? Roo? Would you be so kind as to continue serving Rabbit's friends-and-relations while we talk a little about Spending Time Wisely."

"Oh, yes!" said Tigger. "Serving is what Tiggers do best."

"Can we listen too?" asked Roo.

"Of course," said The Stranger.

Rabbit finally agreed, and having gone into his house and got a large blanket, he and Pooh and Piglet and The Stranger settled down for a talk while Tigger and Roo brought more tea and sandwiches, which of

course made Pooh happy, and The Stranger began to explain.

"What is Time?" asked The Stranger.

"Something I have arrived just in," said Owl, flying in from the direction of his house. "I heard from one of Rabbit's friends-and-relations who had to leave early that you were gathering for a discourse. I came straight along to assist."

"Well, thank you, Owl," said The Stranger. "We were just starting. We began by asking, 'What is Time?'"

No one offered an answer. And Owl, who had just arrived, was fidgeting and adjusting his perch, pretending not to have heard the question.

"Well, let's start this way," said The Stranger. "What does time do?"

"Time passes," said Pooh.

"Time races," said Roo.

"Time flies!" squealed Piglet.

"Time stands still," groaned Eeyore. "When it's not marching on."

"Does that tell us what time is?" asked The Stranger.

"It's what comes in between things," said Pooh, "to keep them from all happening at once."

"Very good, Pooh," said The Stranger. "I think that's a very interesting way of putting it. Now, many people have written books and proposed theories about Time Management, and the first thing we should say is that you cannot Manage Time!"

They looked at one another.

"I repeat, you cannot Manage Time!" said The Stranger.

Pooh ate his last watercress sandwich, trying to keep his strength up, as it now seemed he might need it.

"Then . . . uh . . ." stammered Piglet, "why are we here?"

"As we said before," explained The Stranger, "time flies and it passes and races. We cannot control time, so what we must do is manage the way we *use* our time. And *that* is why I like to say 'Spending Time Wisely' and not call our subject 'Time Management.' Spending Time Wisely means using the time you have in the most effective way to accomplish the things that you want to do."

Pooh sighed and let out a breath as he reached for another sandwich.

"Many people talk about time," continued The Stranger, "as though it were money. They talk about buying it and saving it and spending it. And while these are mostly forms of speech, it is important to remember that each and every one of us has the same amount of time each day to do what we like. It is *how* you use that time that can make a difference in Accomplishing your Goals.

"You remember that we started our talks about Success by Selecting a Dream and Using Your Dream to Set a Goal. We then Create a Plan to achieve our goal, Consider Resources that are available and that would be needed. We then Enhance Skills and Abilities to improve our performance and have come to the next step in the Success program. In this step we will improve our use of time so that we spend our most productive time, and the greatest amount of time, on those things from our Plan that will bring us closer to our Goals. Do you all understand?"

"No," said Rabbit. "I've got too many things to do to worry about which things I should be doing to be able to do the things I want!"

"Rabbit, this talk will be especially for you," said The Stranger. "Because you always find yourself so busy, you will benefit the most from what I have to say.

"What do you think you do with your time?" asked The Stranger.

"I don't think," said Rabbit, "I *know!*"

"I don't think you know either," said Eeyore.

The Stranger laughed, and said to Rabbit, "Tell us about one of your busy days."

It was going to be one of Rabbit's busy days. As soon as he woke up he felt important, as if everything depended upon him. It was just the day for Organizing Something, or for Writing a Notice Signed Rabbit, or for Seeing What Everybody Else Thought About It. It was a perfect morning for hurrying round to Pooh, and saying, "Very well, then, I'll tell Piglet," and then going to Piglet, and saying, "Pooh thinks—but perhaps I'd better see Owl first." It was a Captainish sort of day, when everybody said, "Yes, Rabbit" and "No, Rabbit," and waited until he had told them.

He came out of his house and sniffed the warm spring morning as he wondered what he would do. Kanga's house was nearest, and at Kanga's house was Roo,

"That's Me!" said Roo.

. . . who said "Yes, Rabbit" and "No, Rabbit" almost better than anybody else in the Forest; but there was another animal there nowadays, the strange and Bouncy Tigger;

"That's Me!" said Tigger.

. . . and he was the sort of Tigger who was always in front
when you were showing him the way anywhere, and was
generally out of sight when at last you came to the place
and said proudly "Here we are!"

"No, not Kanga's," said Rabbit thoughtfully to himself, as he curled his whiskers in the sun; and, to make
quite sure that he wasn't going there, he turned to the
left and trotted off in the other direction, which was the
way to Christopher Robin's house.

"Thank you, Rabbit," said The Stranger. "So we
see that on that particular morning, you started off to

go to Christopher Robin's house before you had quite decided what it was you were going to do that day."

"Is that bad?" asked Pooh.

"Well, not bad," said The Stranger. "But if we are interested in making better use of the time we have, we want to try to spend it on the things that are most important to us."

"But I seem to be so busy now," said Rabbit. "Why, I could barely get by if I were to stay up all night to get things done."

"That brings up an Important Point," said The Stranger. "When we are talking about Spending Time Wisely, we will be looking at ways of making better use of the time you normally use for work or play. While you might be tempted, as Rabbit has just said, to get additional time to do things by using time you normally reserve for eating and sleeping, this is Not Suggested. This time, called 'subsistence time,' is *not* part of what we are concerned with here. It would not be right to cut out sleep or meals or the other things you have to do to gain additional time or to become more effective in using the time you have."

"That's good," said Pooh, obviously relieved.

"One of the ways we *can* start is to examine how we use our time now," said The Stranger. "Taking a close look at how we currently arrange our time and seeing whether it matches up with how we want to spend it, that is, our Goal and the Plan we have created, will give us a place to begin improving our performance."

"What methodology does one employ when examining temporal utilization?" asked Owl.

"And *how* do we examine our time use?" asked Roo.

"One of the best ways," said The Stranger, "is to keep a log of your time use for a period of time, usually a week. Keep track of the different things that you spend time doing and how long you spend on each one. Once you have completed the time log you can review it to see if you are spending your time the way you thought you were. Your findings here will help you later on to address the areas where you think you may be able to save time."

"But I thought you said before that you couldn't *save* time?" asked Piglet.

"You're right, Piglet," said The Stranger. "You *can't* save time in the sense that you can store it. But I mean save time in the sense that any time that I do *not* use on things that aren't important to me, is time I *can* spend on things that are. That is what I meant by saving time."

"I see," said Piglet knowingly.

"Once you have examined your time," continued The Stranger, "and have reviewed your current use of time against your Goal and your Plan, you have probably found several areas that could be improved or that are problems for you. For example, ways that you are spending your time that you would like to eliminate or things that are difficult and time-consuming to do, but shouldn't be. Now, we can talk about several different things you can do to save time, and you know what I mean by that, don't you, Piglet?"—and at this point Piglet nodded excitedly—"and to improve the way that you use time. Here, let me write them down for you to look at."

The Stranger took a pad of paper from his pocket and wrote up a list of things, and it looked like this:

Schedule to allow time for individuality, creativity, and flexibility

Achieve results in minimum time by using problem solving

Negate interruptions and minimize routine work

Delegate tasks to others

Share tasks with others—division of labor, teamwork

"These are the things we can do—"

"Look! Look! It spells 'sands'!" squeaked Piglet excitedly.

"No, Piglet," said The Stranger. "This is not one of those. That's just accidental."

"The Sands of Time, no doubt," said Eeyore.

"It's a crow limb," said Pooh proudly.

"That's acronym," said The Stranger.

By this time Piglet and Roo had clasped hands and were dancing around in a circle chanting, "Sands, sands."

"But I'm telling you it's not—well, all right," said The Stranger. "If it helps you to remember, then I guess it's all right to look at it that way. Now the first thing we do is to 'Schedule to allow time for individuality, creativity, and flexibility.' "

"What do you mean by scheduling time for individuality?" asked Pooh, looking very confuzzled.

"Each of us has times during the day," said The Stranger, "when we are more attentive and better able to accomplish difficult things. Just as we also have times when we are less attentive and focused. Sometimes people think of themselves as being 'morning people' if they feel more active in the mornings, and 'night people' if they find they get more done after the sun goes down."

"I am most definitely a night person," said Owl.

"I'm a day person!" chirped Roo.

"I," said Pooh, "am more of an Elevenses person."

"Some things are best done at certain times," said Piglet. When The Stranger asked him what he meant, Piglet told him about the time that he and Pooh were hunting Woozles, and a new Woozle had just joined the others they were tracking.

"Do you see, Piglet? Look at their tracks! Three, as it were, Woozles, and one, as it were, Wizzle. *Another Woozle has joined them!*"

And so it seemed to be. There were the tracks; crossing over each other here, getting muddled up with each other there; but, quite plainly every now and then, the tracks of four sets of paws.

"I *think*," said Piglet, when he had licked the tip of his nose too, and found that it brought very little comfort, "I *think* that I have just remembered something that I forgot to do yesterday and shan't be able to do tomorrow. So I suppose I really ought to go back and do it now."

"We'll do it this afternoon, and I'll come with you," said Pooh.

"It isn't the sort of thing you can do in the afternoon," said Piglet quickly. "It's a very particular morning thing, that has to be done in the morning, and, if possible, between the hours of—What would you say the time was?"

"About twelve," said Winnie-the-Pooh, looking at the sun.

"Between, as I was saying, the hours of twelve and twelve five. So, really, dear old Pooh, if you'll excuse me—*What's that?*"

"Was it a Woozle?" asked Roo, excitedly.

"No," said Piglet. "It was Christopher Robin. You see, some things are Very Particular morning kinds of things."

"When you are scheduling your time," said The Stranger, "and you are going to place the most important or difficult work at your 'best' times, it is important not to schedule *all* your time. That means that you don't need to worry about every second. This is done for two reasons. First, many things take longer to do than you expect. So when you are scheduling, you should be flexible and allow for that. The other reason is that many of the things we want to do require creativity. And while a discussion of creativity could easily take all day, suffice it to say here that we want to allow some time, too, for Free Thinking and Pursuing New Ideas."

"Like new ways to get Honey from the Bee Tree?" asked Pooh.

"Have you thought of some?" asked The Stranger.

"Well, no," said Pooh. "But that is one of my Goals."

"So we schedule our time," continued The Stranger, "so that we are working on the most important things during the times when we are at our best. And we remember to allow flexibility in our schedule and set aside time for creative purposes. The next thing we can do is to 'Achieve results in minimum time by using problem solving.' You remember when we talked about using Problem Solving not just to solve problems, but also as a way of improving processes."

"Work Simplification," said Owl.

"Yes, Owl," said The Stranger. "Work Simplification is the application of Problem Solving to a process or a task in a special way. We set our problem to be 'How to perform the task using less effort or money,' or in this case, less time. When we then solve the problem, we find a quicker way to do it, and that means we will have more time to spend on other things."

"We've saved time!" said Piglet. "In a special sense, of course."

"The next thing we can do to try to improve the use of our time," said The Stranger, "is to 'Negate interruptions and minimize routine work.' Have you ever tried to do something—"

"Could you please pass the sandwiches," said Pooh.

"As I was saying," said The Stranger, "have you ever tried to do something, only to be interrupted—"

"And just a little more tea, Tigger," said Pooh.

"—only to be interrupted, over and over ag—"

"You don't suppose there's a small bit of honey to—"

"Pooh!"

"Oh. I'm sorry, I wasn't quite listening," said Pooh. "Please do go ahead."

"Thank you," said The Stranger. "Interruptions are one of the ways that can keep you from being effective at using your time. Every time you are interrupted, you must stop what you are doing and apply yourself to whatever it is that interrupted you, whether a phone call or even just someone saying 'Hi,' before you can return to what it was you were doing in the first place. Many activities require concentration without interruptions. Whether it is work, or study or reading or whatever, each time you are interrupted, you must begin again to concentrate."

"Like when I'm humming new hums to myself," said Pooh. "I generally like to do it all at once. But if I am interrupted, like by lunch or something, sometimes I have to wait for them to come to me again."

"Exactly," said The Stranger. "So if you can, it is wise to try to set aside blocks of time when you are not to be bothered so that you can concentrate. And while everyone must be available to his friends and coworkers some of the time, if you can control your interruptions—"

"As opposed to them controlling you," added Eeyore.

"Yes. Thank you, Eeyore," said The Stranger. "As

opposed to them controlling you, you will find you can get a great deal more done, and thereby save yourself some time. Minimizing routine work is also something that can help you save time. Routine work is anything that is done the same way, over and over again, but cannot be eliminated. This can be filling out forms or filing papers, or anything which you *must* do, but that is generally done the same way each time. Finding ways to make this work go more quickly, or, if possible, eliminating it altogether, gives you more time to spend on other activities."

"Would this apply to something like washing dishes?" asked Rabbit, looking around at all of his friends-and-relations and all of the cups and plates that were now lying dirty as a result of their Tea.

"It could," said The Stranger. "You might consider consolidating a lot of dishes and washing them once a day instead of after each meal. Or perhaps an automatic dishwasher would save some time." Rabbit wondered who The Stranger was referring to and whether he was free this afternoon. "Or perhaps you would consider using disposable dishes that don't need to be washed at all."

"Oh, it's much too late for that," said Rabbit, looking around at the others.

"Any of these ideas could help save you some time," said The Stranger. "Another idea that is also very powerful is the next one on our list, which is 'Delegate tasks to others.' When you are able to delegate activities to others for completion, it allows you—except for checking on how things are going every once in a while—to move on to doing something else."

"Just like I did this time when I told Rabbit to tell the others about this meeting," said Pooh.

"Well, not quite," said Eeyore. "As Rabbit didn't tell anyone. And no one came. Sounds like my birthday, if you ask me."

"That's true, Eeyore," said The Stranger. "And that's why we said that when you delegate something to someone else to do, it is often very wise and useful to check and see how things are going, in case there are problems."

"Or someone forgets," added Piglet, still upset with Rabbit for not having been invited to the Tea.

"Our last technique," said The Stranger, "for saving time is to 'Share tasks with others—division of labor, teamwork.' And this, too, like Delegation, can be a very powerful tool for saving time and effectively achieving your goals. If you are able to have others help you with the activities you need to accomplish, you can get much more done than if you were to do them yourself. The old saying that 'Many hands make light work' can be a great way to save time and become more effective at pursuing your goals."

"Is that why Alexander Beetle can lift fir cones almost as big as he is?" asked Tigger. "Because he has so many hands?"

"I'm sure that's part of it," said The Stranger. "But I'm not sure that's all there is to it. When we ask others to help us, we can ask people who have skills and capabilities that we don't have. Remember the talk that we had on Considering Resources and how some of the resources could be people? In that way our team can have much greater abilities than each individual alone does."

"But how do you get them to do that?" asked Rabbit. "Why would they want to when it's not even their dishes or anything?"

"Sometimes people will help you just because you ask," said The Stranger. "Or you may hire someone to participate in a team you are creating. Recall our talks on Management? Perhaps you can show them how they can benefit from helping you. They could become part of the effort for what they themselves hoped to get out of it. There are many different ways of sharing work and creating teams, although they usually work best when all the members of the team will benefit from their combined accomplishments."

"I still don't understand how," said Rabbit.

"Let me show you," said The Stranger.

The Stranger stood up and began picking up the plates and cups that they had used for their Tea. After a moment, Tigger began to help too. Not because he understood what The Stranger was doing, but just because it was the kind of thing that Tiggers were best at. It was Piglet who was the first to understand, probably because of his schooling, and he, too, began to help The Stranger and Tigger to clean up. Soon Pooh and Eeyore and even some of Rabbit's friends-and-relations pitched in, all except for Owl, who didn't think his Necessary Dorsal Muscles were quite up to the task.

It didn't take long to clear up all the dishes, take them into Rabbit's house (although The Stranger almost became as stuck as Pooh had once been in Rabbit's front door), and wash them and dry them and put them away. The Stranger and the others finished their work and rejoined Owl and Rabbit outside.

"There," said The Stranger. "That didn't take long. And I hope that I proved my point, Rabbit. When you share tasks with others—oh, and thank you all for your help—they go more quickly and are easier to do."

"Thank you so much," said Rabbit. "I see what you mean. Instead of spending the rest of the day cleaning up I shall be able to . . . uh . . . I've forgotten just what it is I have to do next!"

"There's one other thing that is useful to know when we are talking about Spending Time Wisely," said The Stranger, "and that is the fact that any activity is made up of three parts." He again took out his pad and wrote:

Preparing to do the activity

Performing the activity

Putting everything away after the activity is
   completed

"Aha!" said Piglet. "The three P's!"

"Not again," said The Stranger.

"Is that like the Five W's?" asked Owl.

"I think it must be," said Pooh.

"The reason why this can be helpful is that many tasks and activities take less time to do than they take to get ready for, and to clean up after."

"Like having friends-and-relations over to tea," said Rabbit.

"Precisely," said The Stranger. "So if you are

having everyone over for tea, and you can find some
way to reduce the amount of time you must spend preparing for them or in putting everything away after-
ward—"

"Like having everyone help clean the dishes,"
squeaked Roo.

"—it can save you time to spend on other things,"
said The Stranger.

"And it will let you spend the greatest amount of
time having tea and eating sandwiches!" said Pooh.

"So remember," said The Stranger, "for any activity, look for ways to reduce the time spent getting ready
and cleaning up to maximize the time you spend *doing*
so you can—"

"Save Time!" cried Piglet.

"Perhaps we can spend just a moment talking about
what we have learned," said The Stranger. "We talked
about what time was and how you cannot manage time
at all, you can only manage your *use* of time. We said
the best place to look for ways to save time—"

"In a very special sense of the word," added Piglet.

"—is to look at the time you now spend working
or playing, and not to cut down on the necessary time
spent on eating and sleeping and taking care of yourselves. The best way to start, we said, is to find out
how you use your time now. If you can keep a record
of how you use your time for a one-week period, you
can learn a great deal about how you currently use your

time and by comparing it against your Goal and your Plan, see whether it matches how you would *like* to spend your time."

"Although you can't really spend it," said Pooh.

"And then we discussed ways to save time," said The Stranger.

"Sands!" shouted Roo and Piglet together.

"Yes. Sands," said The Stranger. "Which includes Scheduling to work on our most important priorities during the times when we are at our best. While remembering, of course, that we want to be flexible about our scheduling, as things usually take longer than we expect, and also to allow time to be creative and spontaneous.

"Next," continued The Stranger, "we try to Achieve results in the minimum time and use what we learned from Problem Solving to find the easiest and quickest way to do those things. We can also become more effective by Negating interruptions and minimizing repetitive work. And that brings us to two other techniques, Delegation and Division of work. Using Delegation, we can take activities that need to be done and have someone else work on them. This saves our time—"

"Except for checking up to Make Sure," said Piglet.

"—to spend on other activities. And when we talk about Division of work, we mean Sharing tasks with others, which we can do by enlisting other people's help or by creating teams to complete activities. And we said that besides having others to help you accomplish the work, you can also access different skills and capabilities depending on who is helping."

"Whew! That's a lot," said Pooh.

"Yes it is, Pooh," said The Stranger. "And there's just one more thing we discussed, and that was the fact that most activities can be broken down into Preparation, Performance, and Putting Away—"

"The Three P's!" said Piglet.

"—and that anything we can do to reduce preparation time and cleanup allows us more time to work on the Performance part. Which is the most effective part of any task. I want to thank you all for listening—"

"All done? Good!" said Rabbit. "I really shouldn't have taken all of this time out, but just the same, thank you."

And off he went, stopping at each of the groups of his friends-and-relations, asking about whether they had enjoyed their tea, whether there was anything they needed, and so on. By the time he had reached his own front door he was just as busy and filled with importance and undone errands as he had been before.

"I shall have to be going," said The Stranger. "I want to thank you all for listening today. I hope that you learned something useful and that it is helpful to

you. Now I must return to
the village, as I have some
things I must do.

"Well, what do you think,
Eeyore?" said The Stranger.
"Do you think you'll be able
to use some of the things we
talked about here today?"

"Not in a donkey's years," grumbled Eeyore. "But
it's not your fault. I think you explained it well. I think
I am just rather timeless."

"I think so too, Eeyore," said The Stranger.

"It doesn't look as if Rabbit learned much either,"
said Piglet, watching Rabbit as he rushed back and
forth to his guests, as busy and distracted as he was
when they arrived.

"You know, Pooh," said The Stranger, "changing
habits and doing things a new way, even if it is a Better
Way, is difficult for many. It may seem that you are
not progressing at all as you are trying out some of the
new ways to do things that we talked about. But if you
are patient and persistent, you will be rewarded by having more control over your time, and by accomplishing
those things that are most important to you, and that
will move you toward your Goal."

"Yes," said Pooh, looking at Rabbit. "These things
do indeed take time."

VIII

In which A Game of Cloud Shapes
Is Interrupted, Everyone Starts
to Achieve Success, and Rabbit and
Pooh Give Lessons

It was a drowsy sort of day. It was a day when an Un-seasonably Warm South wind surprised everyone in the Hundred Acre Wood and made them think it was certainly Spring and maybe even Summer.

It was a Lie-on-Your-Back-on-the-Grass-and-Look-Up-at-Towering-Snow-White-Clouds kind of day. It was the kind of day when it seemed doing Nothing was better than doing Something.

Actually, Pooh and Piglet and Rabbit were doing something. They had, it is true, started off doing nothing but lying in the grass at the base of the small hill near what had been Pooh's house and was now Pooh and Piglet's house and enjoying the warm breeze and the sun, but Pooh changed that by saying that the shape of a cloud reminded him of a jar of honey. Piglet piped up, saying that the cloud a little closer to the horizon bore a remarkable resemblance to a pile of Hay-corns ready to be stored for Winter. Rabbit joined in by pointing out how much the small cloud just above the one that Piglet had mentioned looked like Alexander Beetle.

Before anyone knew it they were deep in a game of Cloud Shapes. Rabbit was winning, because he had far more friends-and-relations that clouds could look like than either Pooh or Piglet had, and since nobody but Rabbit knew all of them they had to take Rabbit's word that a certain cloud looked like one specific friend-or-relation.

In truth, if one had to do Something on such a drowsy day, it was a very suitable sort of game. Much less tiring than Poohsticks, since it didn't even involve having to run from one side of the bridge to the other, nor did they need to go to the Poohsticks Bridge. They could play the game right outside Pooh's. Where they were, as it was.

The Stranger appeared at the top of the hill just when they were trying to decide if a certain cloud looked more like a large version of Small or a castle. This was difficult because none of them had a very good idea of what a castle looked like. From time to time Christopher Robin had mentioned a castle, but he had never actually described what a castle looked like. Pooh tried to settle it by saying that a castle looked very much like a large version of Small, but Rabbit disagreed, saying that he was reasonably sure that a castle was something that you lived in and that even a large version of Small wouldn't be suitable to live in.

The question of the castle or Small never did get decided because The Stranger interrupted the game by coming down the hill and sitting down beside them in the grass and the warm sunshine. He was soon followed by the other dwellers in the Hundred Acre Wood, who did the same.

It was such a lazy, drowsy, do-nothing sort of day that the greetings and the hallos were very subdued and even Tigger was not his usual bouncy self. It was some time before The Stranger stirred himself and sat up.

"I suppose that we ought to start," he said, not sounding as though he really meant it.

"Start what?" asked Pooh, who was sort of wondering if he ought to sit up and see if The Stranger had brought a smackerel and if that was what he was proposing to start.

"We were going to talk about the last and the most important step in the process you can use to pursue and achieve Success."

"Oh," said Pooh, not very interested since it didn't seem to involve a smackerel. "Today, I think I'd rather lie in the grass and look at clouds. It doesn't seem like the kind of day to pursue and achieve much of anything." He paused and thought for a moment. "Could we start tomorrow? Unless tomorrow is the same sort of day. In which case we might want to put things off until seventeen days come Friday."

The Stranger sighed, then looked up at the blue sky and the white clouds and then at everyone lying on the grassy hill.

"Pooh," The Stranger said, "I can understand why you feel that way. You've just given us a good example of why we have the last step in our Success Formula."

"I have?" said Pooh, uncertain whether that was a Good Thing or a Bad Thing. Pooh paused and scratched his head, trying to think. "I forget what you said the last step is. Bother! I fear I am a Bear of Very Little Brain."

"It starts with an S," volunteered Roo, who remembered and who had been learning his letters from Owl and Kanga.

"That's exactly right, Roo," said The Stranger. Owl and Kanga looked proudly at Roo. "The last and most important step in our process of achieving success is Start!"

"Oh," said Pooh. "I should have remembered."

"You see, Pooh," The Stranger continued, "by wanting to put off learning the last step you did what many people do: putting off the process of achieving success. One can always find an excuse to do that. It is so common that it even has a name—'procrastination.' "

"Procrustean nations?" said Pooh.

"Procrastination, Pooh Bear," said Owl. "Putting off until later what should be done now."

"There are many reasons why people procrastinate," said The Stranger. "It could be that all at once it seems like a lot of trouble and work; they might fail (if they don't start, they can't fail); doing something new almost always involves change, and change for many individuals is threatening; and so on.

"This is why Start is the most important step in the process. If you don't start to carry out the plan that you have conceived and developed, you won't reach your goal."

"Logically irrefutable and an intrinsically unimpeachable proposition," said Owl.

"I can understand that," said Pooh. "But what I don't understand is how to Start. That sounds like a 'What' to me. I need a 'How.' "

"Well, it's really quite simple," said The Stranger. "You just Get Organized and Go!"

"I know about Organization," said Rabbit. "I can remember several things that I organized. One of them was a Search." Rabbit paused. "Searches almost always have to be Organized."

"What's Org . . . Organ . . . Organi . . . What you said?" Piglet asked The Stranger.

"Why don't you tell us about the Search, Rabbit?" The Stranger suggested. "Maybe that will help us learn what 'Get Organized' involves."

"I remember it," volunteered Owl.

Pooh was sitting in his house one day counting his pots of honey, when there came a knock on the door.

"Fourteen," said Pooh. "Come in. Fourteen. Or was it fifteen? Bother. That's muddled me."

"Hallo, Pooh," said Rabbit.

"Hallo, Rabbit. Fourteen, wasn't it?"

"What was?"

"My pots of honey what I was counting."

"Fourteen, that's right."

"Are you sure?"

"No," said Rabbit. "Does it matter?"

"I just like to know," said Pooh humbly. "So as I can say to myself: 'I've got fourteen pots of honey left.' Or fifteen, as the case may be. It's sort of comforting."

"Well, let's call it sixteen," said Rabbit. "What I came to say was: Have you seen Small anywhere about?"

"I don't think so," said Pooh. And then, after thinking a little more, he said: "Who is Small?"

"One of my friends-and-relations," said Rabbit carelessly.

This didn't help Pooh very much, because Rabbit had so many friends-and-relations, and of such different sorts and sizes, that he didn't know whether he ought to be looking for Small at the top of an oak-tree or in the petal of a buttercup.

"I haven't seen anybody today," said Pooh, "not so as to say 'Hallo, Small,' to. Did you want him for anything?"

"I *don't* want him," said Rabbit. "But it's always useful to know where a friend-and-relation *is*, whether you want him or whether you don't."

"Oh, I see," said Pooh. "Is he lost?"

"Well," said Rabbit, "nobody has seen him for a long time, so I suppose he is. Anyhow," he went on importantly, "I promised Christopher Robin I'd Organize a Search for him, so come on."

Pooh said good-bye affectionately to his fourteen pots of honey, and hoped they were fifteen; and he and Rabbit went out into the Forest.

"Now," said Rabbit, "this is a Search, and I've Organized it—"

"Done what to it?" said Pooh.

"Organized it. Which means—well, it's what you do to a Search, when you don't all look in the same place at once. So I want *you*, Pooh, to search by the Six Pine Trees first, and then work your way towards Owl's House, and look out for me there. Do you see?"

"No," said Pooh. "What—"

"Then I'll see you at Owl's House in about an hour's time."

"Is Piglet organdized too?"

"We all are," said Rabbit, and off he went.

"So that was it," concluded Owl.

"Actually," said Pooh, "there was more. I had to organdize myself first, so I wrote down in my head the Order of Looking for Things, so I could find Small. Which I did. Find Small that is."

"And there was lots more," said Piglet quickly. "Pooh falling into a piece of the Forest which had been left out by mistake and me finding him, and Pooh deciding it was a Heffalump Trap and—"

"I remember it now, Piglet," said The Stranger. "It was a long adventure and later you can tell us the rest of it, but now I'd like to concentrate on the How of Starting by talking about how to Get Organized and Go! Why do we want to get organized?"

"That's obvious," said Rabbit. "Without Organization you don't get things done, or at least they don't get done as well and as quickly." He went on before anyone could interrupt. "Most important of all is that you need someone to be in charge. Someone who has had experience. Like someone who organized not only the Search for Small, but How to Deal with Strange Animals in the Forest and the Way to Unbounce a Tigger and—"

"That's very good, Rabbit," interrupted The Stranger. "You mentioned the very reason why the last and most important step in our procedure for achieving success should be 'Start. Get Organized and Go!' "

"The reason is that Rabbit should Organdize things?" said Pooh, who hadn't really been paying close attention.

Rabbit was about to say that Pooh was absolutely right, but The Stranger spoke first.

"No," said The Stranger. "As Rabbit mentioned, the reason is that by organizing you get things done better and more quickly. You see, up to this point we've talked and learned about selecting a dream that you want to achieve; using your dream to set a goal; creating a plan to achieve your goal; identifying the resources that you have available to carry out the steps in the plan; identifying and acquiring those resources that you don't have but need and how to best use and most effectively spend your time to achieve your goal."

"To achieve Success," squeaked Roo to show he was still listening even if it was a drowsy sort of day.

"However you define it," said Pooh, not to be outdone.

"Precisely," said The Stranger. "All of those steps could be considered to be part of organizing to achieve success. Now, to be certain that we understand what we are talking about, can anyone tell me the meanings of 'organization' and 'organize'?"

"There is, I think," said Owl, "a definition for each that would be appropriate and germane to the present discussion and meet the insinuated parameters. We might say that 'Organization' is a noun and can be defined as 'a systematic arrangement for a definite purpose.' 'Organize,' a transitive verb, is to put one's self in a state of mental competence to perform a task."

"Excellent, Owl!" said The Stranger. "Just the definitions that are wanted."

Owl preened his feathers, pleased at the praise but not wanting to show it. He was also particularly pleased with identifying the word classifications, since he had been brushing up on parts of speech while teaching Roo his letters.

"We can use Rabbit's and Pooh's adventure in the Search for Small to illustrate the definitions," The Stranger continued. "There is something that you should remember: Organization is not an objective or a goal, it is a way to achieve a goal or an objective. You should keep your organization as simple as possible as long as you can use it to reach your objective."

"Success," squeaked Roo, having had that well received the last time, or at least no one had said, "Now, Roo."

The Stranger nodded. "Can anyone tell me what Rabbit and Christopher Robin's objective or goal was in the adventure?"

"To find Small," said Eeyore. "Not an easy thing to do, as I well know. One must always watch where one puts one's hoof or else one might make an unfortunate impression on Small. Not to mention that you could go on searching for two days if no one told you that Small had been found."

"Good," said The Stranger. "Now you will notice that Rabbit followed the steps we have talked about. He established his goal, developed a plan, evaluated and identified his resources—"

"That was us," said Piglet. "Pooh and me and the others who could help search."

"—and assigned the searchers in a way that used everyone's time wisely by making certain that there was no duplication in the areas to be searched. He was therefore making a systematic arrangement for a definite purpose. In other words, he was beginning to achieve his goal by carrying out the last step of our formula."

"What I said," said Owl.

"In addition," The Stranger continued, "Pooh illustrated the second definition because he wrote down in his head the Order of Looking for Things. Putting it another way, he put himself in a state of mental competence to perform a task."

"And I did that without even knowing what it was that I was doing," said Pooh proudly. "It just seemed the Thing to Do."

"Good, Pooh," said The Stranger. "Ideally we would like our efforts to achieve success to be almost second nature, and this is why we begin or start with organizing that process. As you are getting ready to begin, review the steps you have accomplished to make certain that they are applicable and that no revisions are necessary, and that you are ready to begin, and remember to keep things as simple as you can. Check to make certain your resources are available when needed.

"Now," The Stranger continued, "there is another area for organization that I want to talk about. Making certain that you have followed through on all the steps in the Success Formula is vital, and beginning your process of achieving success by putting yourself in a state of mental competence to perform the task gives you a great head start. However, most of the time the process of achieving your goal will be carried out over a relatively long period of time. Usually there is a singular place where most of the work is done to carry out the tasks necessary to achieve your goal.

"If that place, whether it is in a room of your own, a garage, a corner of your desk at work, or at school, is uncomfortable and does not meet your needs, there is a temptation to avoid using it, or if you do use it, for your time spent there to be less productive.

"Depending on your goal your place could be at work, or, increasingly in today's society, at home. Wherever it is, it will pay large dividends if you make certain that the workspace that you will be using in your pursuit of success is well organized, properly equipped, and effectively arranged."

Owl interrupted, "I've read that if you pay attention to the ergonomic aspects of the workplace you will quite possibly avoid thoracic outlet syndrome, neck and back strain, carpal tunnel syndrome, and other ills usually classified as CTDs or cumulative trauma disorders." Owl peered closely at The Stranger. "This is particularly important for a writer," he said sternly.

"That's true," said The Stranger. "Thank you, Owl.

"Organizing your workplace is a big subject but there are many books that will give you an idea of how you should go about doing so."

"I don't think I would be able to become a writer," said Eeyore gloomily, looking down at his hoofs. "I think I'm digitally challenged when it comes to typing, although I did make an A once. You don't need a keyboard for that—three sticks will do. Piglet saw me."

Eeyore sighed and looked around for a thistle. Not seeing any, he sighed again. "This selecting a goal and being a success is difficult. For the moment I think I'd settle for a thistle." He paused and thought a moment.

"A tender, succulent one would be nice, however, not just any old sat-upon-thrashed-about kind of thistle."

"It may be true," said The Stranger, "that achieving success is something that is difficult, but I think you'll find that using the Success Formula makes it easier and more enjoyable and gives you a better chance to get what you want out of life."

Pooh settled back down in the grass and looked up at the clouds drifting by high overhead. "Right now," he said, "I think I'd settle for just doing this as success."

"We don't want to procrastinate," said The Stranger, settling down beside Pooh. "But I think we've covered enough material on a lazy, drowsy day like this and there is nothing wrong with a well-earned break, particularly when it is almost time for elevenses and I have a few smackerels in my basket."

The others settled down also as The Stranger got out the smackerels.

"I still think it looks like a castle," said Piglet, looking up at the clouds.

"Or like Small," said Rabbit.

"Who?" said Owl.

"Not 'Who,' Owl," said Pooh sleepily. " 'How.' "

"How to Start is Get Organized and Go!" squeaked Piglet.

"Hooray!" shouted Roo, who was anxious to begin working to be a success.

IX

IN WHICH Pooh Goes Missing, The Stranger Comes to the Rescue, and the Success Formula Is Employed

The Stranger stopped packing his bags and stared out of the open window of his room at the Inn toward the Forest. It had been three days since he had last seen his friends. He had been writing down all of the things they had been talking about.

As he was zipping up his last bag, Owl flew and perched on the window.

"Oh, . . . huff, huff, . . . I'm so glad . . . that I caught you," Owl said.

"What is it, Owl?" said The Stranger.

"It's Pooh, huff, huff," said Owl, "or rather, it's *not* Pooh. Actually, it's more of a where than a what. . . ."

"What do you mean?" asked The Stranger.

"Pooh's gone missing!"

"Oh my goodness," said The Stranger.

"Yes. It has been an entire day since anyone has

seen him," said Owl. "It's just not like him at all to be gone so long. You must come and help us search."

So The Stranger left the Inn and hurried along after Owl, who flew straight to the Forest.

"I have asked all the others to meet us at Pooh's house," said Owl as he flew on above The Stranger.

When Owl and The Stranger arrived at Pooh's house, everyone was there. Eeyore was munching on some thistles nearby; Piglet was running about asking everyone three times if they had seen Pooh; and Rabbit was busy trying to make everyone comfortable and keep his friends-and-relations out of trouble.

"Here they are!" shouted Piglet.

And with that, The Stranger began to speak to each of the animals and eventually came to understand that Pooh had last been seen two days before. Alexander Beetle had spied him near Owl's house, walking toward Piglet's, humming, and carrying a large pot. That was all.

"What shall we do?" asked Piglet, whose ears were twitching more than when Heffalumps were about.

"We shall find him, Piglet," said The Stranger. "Please don't worry. You know how Pooh is. He probably just wandered off on one of his adventures. With the right kind of search, I'm certain we should be seeing him again before noon."

But The Stranger was wrong. The Stranger helped split everyone into search parties. Eeyore and Roo were

sent to Eeyore's Gloomy place, Rabbit and his friends-
and-relations went to the Bee Tree and the Big Stones
and Rocks, Kanga and Tigger went to the Sandy Pit,
Owl flew to the Six Pine Trees and then on to the
Hundred Acre Wood, and Piglet and The Stranger
went to Piglet's house and then to the Heffalump trap
(just in case). They were all to meet after the Search
(including Pooh, who was certain to be found).

"Where shall we meet?" asked Piglet. "Once we
have found Pooh Bear, of course."

"Let's meet at the Bee Tree!" said Tigger.

"Owl's house," said Owl.

"The Sandy Pit!" chirped Roo.

"I think," said The Stranger, "that we should meet
somewhere that is in the middle of our Search Area.
That way it will be easiest for each one of us."

"We can meet at the Lightning Tree," said Piglet. "That is near where the Woozle wasn't and on the way to the Six Pine Trees. Do you all know it?"

In between Piglet's house and Owl's house (which is to say, Owl's new house and Owl's old house) at the edge of the Hundred Acre Wood was a large gray tree that had been struck by lightning. The lightning strike had hollowed out the tree, but left it standing, and it was a prominent and central place to meet.

They agreed to meet just as soon as they had finished covering their areas, and all were convinced that Pooh would be with them when they next met.

But he wasn't.

Owl finished first, as he could cover the most ground rapidly, and he watched as each of the parties arrived at the Lightning Tree and reported their lack of success in finding Pooh. The Stranger and Piglet were the last to arrive, having taken a little extra time to stop in again at Pooh's house just in case he had come home.

"Has anyone found him?" asked Piglet.

"No," said Eeyore, looking especially gloomy. "Not a sign. Not even an empty honey pot."

"You mean like this one?" squeaked Roo.

"What one?" asked The Stranger.

"This one," said Roo, dragging a large, heavy, and decidedly empty honey pot from under a gorse bush next to the Lightning Tree.

"A Clue!" shouted Piglet.

"Where exactly did you find this?" asked The Stranger.

"Why, right here at the base of the tree."

And that was when they heard it.

At first it sounded like the sound the wind makes in the fall when it moans through the woods making everything clear and cold.

"Oooooooo!"

"Did you hear that?" asked Piglet.

"Hearing is what Tiggers do best. Hear what?" said Tigger.

"Oooooooooooo!"

"That!"

"Quick, everybody," said The Stranger, "search around the tree."

They searched.

"Anybody find anything?" asked The Stranger.

"Just this," said Rabbit, holding up a small picnic basket that looked exactly like the one that Pooh would sometimes take with him when he was expecting to be out for the day.

"That's Pooh's!" shouted Piglet.

"A Pooh Clue!" squealed Roo.

"Oooooooooo!"

"I think I have an idea," said The Stranger. He went over to the trunk of the Lightning Tree and rapped loudly three times on the trunk. *Knock, knock, knock!*

Very faintly and somewhat sadly someone said, "Come in."

"It's Pooh! It's you, Pooh!" said Piglet, and he began to run in circles around the base of the tree while Tigger bounced and all the others shouted, "We've found Pooh! Hooray!"

After a few trial shouts they determined that Pooh's voice was coming from a spot about ten feet up in the trunk of the tree, just below the first large branches that ran out from the main trunk.

"However did you get stuck up in that tree?" asked The Stranger.

"It is a long story," said Pooh, sounding somewhat muffled from inside the tree.

"It seems like we have some time," said Eeyore.

"I was trying to be successful," started Pooh. "I wanted to be successful, so I used the approach that The Stranger has been teaching us."

"The Success Formula!" squeaked Piglet.

"Yes," said Pooh. "I started by Selecting a Dream. What a wonderful dream it was. . . ." Here Pooh sighed a sigh that was so loud that all the others standing around the trunk of the Lightning Tree could hear. "It was a dream of honey. Lots of honey. Enough to last a whole summer. Actually, it selected me. But once I had the dream, I knew I must pursue it."

"So what did you do?" asked The Stranger.

"Why, the next step, of course," said Pooh. "I Used My Dream to Set a Goal."

"And what was the goal, kind Bear?" asked Owl.

"I remembered that recently in the Forest, I had heard a very loud buzzing sound," said Pooh. "And where there is buzzing, there are bees—and where there are bees . . ."

"There is honey!" cried Piglet.

"Just so, Piglet," said Pooh. "So I set myself the goal of getting that honey."

"And then," said The Stranger, "you must have Created a Plan, that being the next step."

"Yes, I did," said Pooh, still sounding muffled and sad. "It was a Good Plan. Not very Complex, but Good. First I would go to different parts of the Forest and listen. When I heard the buzzing, I knew I would be close. Then I would listen even more carefully, and find the source of the buzzing, being the tree, the bees, and the honey. Next, I would prepare myself to get the honey and then get it. The honey, that is. And then I would eat it. Well, some of it anyway. If it was really enough to last a whole summer, I would put the rest in my empty jars in my cupboard and . . ."

"Pooh? Are you okay?" asked The Stranger.

"Oh, yes," said the muffled Pooh. "I was just thinking of honey and it made me hungry, so I was just having some."

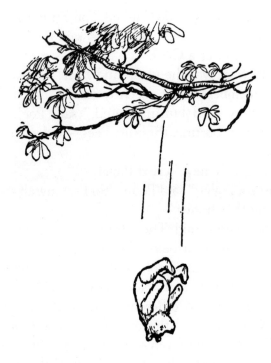

"What happened next?" asked Piglet.

"Well, the next step is Consider Resources," said Pooh. "So that is what I did. I knew that if I were to search for the tree, it might take a long time, so I knew I would need por—, pro—, porvisions . . . something to eat. And I thought I might need some tools to help me scoop up the honey, and jars to carry it in. And I thought, too, it might help if I could climb better. You remember how I fell out of the Bee Tree."

"Falling out of trees is what Tiggers do best," said Tigger.

"So at that point," said Pooh, "I went back and added some climbing practice to my Plan. Just in case, of course. But I knew I had to Enhance my Skills and Abilities if I wanted to get the honey."

"Did you Spend your Time Wisely?" asked The Stranger.

"I did," said Pooh. "I started early, after a good hearty breakfast, as that is the time when I am at my best—after eating, that is. And I planned extra time for practicing my climbing, and finally I made sure not to become distracted, even though I saw a most interesting butterfly on the way. I hope he is still in the Forest when I get out of here. *If* I get out of here."

"Don't worry, Pooh," said The Stranger. "I have been thinking of that while we were talking, and I am sure we can get you out."

"But how?" said Pooh. "It is the 'Hows' that are always the most difficult."

"Perhaps if you finished telling us 'How' you got stuck," said The Stranger, "we might get an idea as to how to get you out."

"We talked about the last step of the process being to Start with Organization," started Pooh. "So I did. I began by organizing all my tools and porvisions and began my Plan. I went to many different parts of the Forest, but it was only when I passed by the Lightning

Tree that I began to hear the buzzing. And it was when I listened more carefully that I realized that it was coming from high up in the tree. So I climbed up and found that the lightning had hollowed out the center of the tree, just right for bees. I was just about to get down and get my jars when I slipped and fell. And here I am, stuck inside. A very sticky stuck. Mmmmmm."

"Don't worry, Pooh," said The Stranger, "we'll get you out."

They all examined Pooh's predicament and discussed different ways of getting Pooh out. Owl thought they might wait until a very blustery day, which would surely knock over the tree, which was not even as strong as the one his house used to be in, but the others thought it wouldn't be right to wait such a long time to rescue Pooh. Eeyore thought they might find a long rope and pull the whole tree down. But they all agreed that might be Dangerous. In the end, they decided they would rescue Pooh in the same way Piglet had got out of Owl's house when it had blown down. They would find a long rope and have Owl fly it up over a branch higher up in the Lightning Tree and then drop the end down to Pooh. All the Others could then pull him up and out of the hollow and he would be Saved. They explained this to Pooh, who only had one problem.

"But how will I get the honey out?"

So while The Stranger went to find the swing they

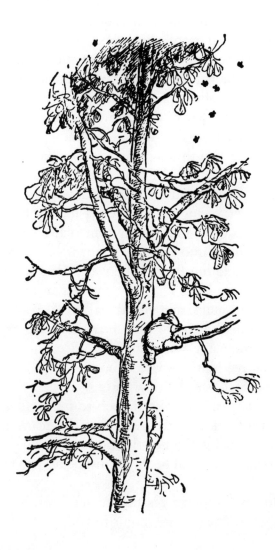

had built earlier, and untied the rope so they could use it to rescue Pooh, Owl flew the empty jars Pooh had brought up to the hollow in the tree, and once Pooh filled them, he pushed them up and out of the hollow and Tigger caught them, using his bounciness to keep them from breaking on the ground. They had filled almost all of the jars by the time The Stranger returned with the rope from the swing.

"Are you sure this is going to work?" asked a muffled Pooh from inside the tree.

"In just one minute we shall have you out," said The Stranger, giving the end of the rope to Owl, who flew it up over a sturdy-looking branch above where Pooh had fallen into the tree.

"Now, hold on, Pooh!" shouted Piglet. "Okay, everybody, *pull!*"

And they pulled and pulled and slowly Pooh's head became visible where the large branches of the tree ran out from the main trunk.

"I can see him!" shouted Roo.

"He's free!" shouted Piglet.

And they gently lowered Pooh to the ground, next to the trunk of the tree and amid the many jars of honey they had got out of the tree.

"Hooray!" shouted Pooh, for his friends had rescued him.

"Hooray!" shouted his friends, for Pooh had been found.

Pooh looked quite a mess, with bits of bark and burrs and honeycomb all stuck to his fur with honey. He thanked each one of his rescuers in turn, and then looked around himself at all the jars of honey lying on the ground.

"I'm a Success!" Pooh shouted.

"Yes. Pooh," said The Stranger. "You did a very good job of following the steps of the Success Formula we have been learning and you have shown that you learned it very well."

"Even if the going got sticky part of the way along," added Eeyore.

"In the future," said The Stranger, "please let someone else know before you go off on an adventure."

"I really hadn't thought it would turn out to be so adventurous," explained Pooh.

"Well I hope you have learned a lesson, Pooh," said The Stranger.

"Oh, yes," said Pooh. "Next time I shall bring even *more* empty jars."

And so The Stranger and Pooh's friends all helped to carry Pooh's honey back to his house. They stopped to put the rope swing back where it had been before, and even took turns on it for a while, just to make sure that it was still working just the way that it had before.

X

IN WHICH The Stranger Reflects on
the Importance of Success
(However You Define It)
and Says Good-bye to His Friends

When The Stranger arrived back at the Inn he was
very tired. But he was also very pleased that he and the
others in the Hundred Acre Wood had been able to
rescue Pooh from his predicament in the Lightning
Tree. The Stranger unpacked his bags, as he would be
staying one more night, and went downstairs to the
Inn's fine bar for a steak-and-kidney pie before retiring.
He placed his order and took a seat at the table nearest
the fireplace.

While he was waiting for his food to be brought,
The Stranger relaxed in the warmth of the fire and
thought about what he had been teaching Pooh and
his friends. From his own experience, he felt confident
that if they had been able to learn even just a little
about how to organize themselves to direct their atten-

tion and efforts toward things that they were indeed interested in, they would be very much the happier for it.

So often, thought The Stranger, people overlook the need to attach a priority to their own dreams, and to act on their dreams. The Stranger thought about his own experiences, and how he had begun working after college, how he had spent years with different companies and in different positions, and how, after a while, he had realized that while he was doing a good job and performing well, there was something missing. He began to look around, at himself and at his work, and observe those things that really interested him and that he truly enjoyed doing. What he decided was that he enjoyed solving problems and working with people and teaching the skills he had acquired to those he worked with.

He had dreamed of how exciting work would be again, if only he could spend all of his time doing just these things. To not have to worry about all the other things he was responsible for, though he could do them reasonably well even though he didn't enjoy them as much, seemed much too good to be true.

The Stranger remembered the day that his boss had called him to headquarters, and how he had curiously felt relieved when he was told that, due to a restructuring and downsizing, his job would be eliminated. He could try to find another position with the company, or he could take a modest severance package. To The Stranger, the choice was obvious.

The Stranger smiled to himself as he also remembered how on the flight home, he had spent the entire time turning his dream into a plan of action. When the plane touched down, he was ready. He spent the last couple of months with the firm working twice as hard as ever putting his plan into action. He called all of his business contacts and explained what he planned to do. When his last day working for the company finally came, he already had several different contracts lined up. Working as a self-employed consultant, he was helping others solve their problems and teaching the techniques to his new clients.

After several years of working on his own, the constant fear of whether or not he could make it on his own faded, and he felt even more confident that the lessons he had learned could, and should, be shared with others.

It was one night, long ago now it seemed, while he was reading a beloved children's story to put his son to sleep, that he conceived of a new dream, the dream of visiting the Forest and meeting his childhood friends and using their adventures in a book to explain and teach the hard-won lessons he had learned.

The Stranger smiled, remembering all of the adventures he and Pooh and Piglet and all the others had been through. The waiter looked at him curiously when he brought the steak-and-kidney pie, no doubt wondering just what it was that was making him smile like a Cheshire cat, but then, that is another story entirely.

The Stranger was also pleased, as he thought that anyone could master the simple tools, techniques, and fundamental principles that were presented in these books that he had been writing, and that they could help anyone to lead a fuller, more enjoyable, satisfying, and productive life. That is, to be more successful (however they defined it and whatever path they followed).

The Stranger remembered how he first met Pooh, and how even then, Pooh was able to put his paw on the crux of the matter.

> Here is Edward Bear, coming downstairs now, bump, bump, bump, on the back of his head, behind Christopher Robin. It is, as far as he knows, the only way of coming downstairs, but sometimes he feels that there really is another way, if only he could stop bumping for a moment and think of it.

The Stranger thought that everyone could benefit from Pooh's advice, and stop bumping for a moment and think of another way.

The Stranger raised his glass in tribute, and said, "Thank you, Pooh, you are a Most Successful Bear."

POOH'S APPENDIX
WINNIE-THE-POOH'S SUCCESS FORMULA

You don't have to have a great memory to be a Success because you can always write things down. Which is what Pooh (sometimes a Very Forgetful Bear) would do if he knew how (it's the "Hows" he has difficulty with).

But Pooh doesn't know how to write, so he uses this reminder to make sure that he stays on the path to success. Since you are the kind of person who is Friendly with Bears, he ever-so-nicely says you may use it also.

EACH INDIVIDUAL MUST DEFINE
WHAT SUCCESS IS
Your Success = S+U+C+C+E+S+S

Select a Dream. Select what you would really like to accomplish, the things you would like to do, or pos-

sibly even an occupation that you would like to follow. Decide what your dreams are, without thinking about obstacles or how difficult they might be to achieve.

Use Your Dream to Set a Goal. A goal is the result toward which effort is directed. There are no limitations on what you may want. To turn a dream into a goal, make the dream specific, concrete, and definite. Example: If the dream is to be rich, the goal might be to have a net worth of $10,317,452.67 within eleven years.

Classify goals as either short-term or long-term (six months or less is short-term).

Don't forget to ACHIEVE:

All of us have possibility power.

Choose your goals carefully because you are going to achieve them.

Have both long- and short-term goals. As you accomplish them, add new ones.

Imagine accomplishing really ambitious goals. (Break intimidating goals down into subgoals that are easier and reward yourself as you reach each subgoal.)

Engendering success requires concrete goals. Be specific when you establish and write down your goals.

Value your long-term goals. The greatest rewards usually come from the achievement of long-term goals.

Eliminate conflict between goals. Establish relative priorities, revising goals or treating conflicts with problem-solving techniques.

Create a Plan. A Plan is a list of the things we need to do, in the right order, that will take us from where we are now to where we want to be.

List individual steps that will move you to your Goal.

Identify the three elements of each step: What, When, and Who.

What is to be done?

Who is going to do it?

When are they going to do it?

Make each part easier and create milestones to measure your progress by breaking the goals down into smaller elements and tasks.

Do not be judgmental.

If a step seems impossible, see if *it* can be broken down into simpler substeps.

A dependent step is one that depends on the completion of a prior step.

Independent steps can usually be done at any time.

Consider Resources. A resource is something that is ready for use or can be drawn upon for aid.

The four main resources are time, money, knowledge, and skills.

Examine your plan and determine the resources required.

Marshal resources or arrange for their availability when needed.

A Skills Inventory is a list of all the things that you know how to do.

- Don't neglect transferability of skills.

- List all the things that you are good at or have experience at doing.

- List only those skills you honestly feel capable of performing.

Review lists (yours and those of others) when you begin a new project or a new job, or when you have a position to fill.

Enhance Skills and Abilities. Your goal may require skills that you don't currently have, or greater abilities than you possess.

Identify what skills and abilities are needed.

To acquire new skills, research what resources are available.

Build your acquisition or practice of skills when you create your plan.

To maintain or improve skills often requires practice.

Practice with purpose.

Practice as often as you can.

Be realistic and patient about progress.

Reward yourself when milestones are achieved.

If you don't have the necessary skills and it is not practical to acquire them yourself, find someone who does and convince him or her to help.

Spend Time Wisely. What is time? "It's what comes in between things," said Pooh, "to keep them from all happening at once."

You cannot Manage Time! Manage the way you *use* your time.

Subsistence time (time to eat, sleep, and play) is *not* to be reduced.

Log and review your current use of time to see if it matches your perceptions.

Ways to improve time usage:

- Schedule to allow time for individuality, creativity, and flexibility.

- Achieve results in minimum time by using problem solving.

- Negate interruptions and minimize routine work.

- Delegate tasks to others.

- Share tasks with others—division of labor, teamwork.

The three parts of any activity:

- Preparing to do the activity.

- Performing the activity.

- Putting everything away after the activity is completed.

Minimize preparation and cleanup for any activity and maximize performance.

Start! Get Organized and Go. The greatest plan in the world is for naught if it is never begun.

To succeed, you must begin. Don't procrastinate!

By organizing, you get things done better and more quickly.

As you are getting ready to begin:

- Review your plan.

- Check to make certain your resources are available when needed.

- Make certain your workspace is well organized, properly equipped, and effectively arranged.

- Your records of the work that you did in selecting your dream, setting your goal, and creating a plan belong at your workspace so that they can be reviewed at regular intervals and adjusted or altered if need be.

- In addition, you should have the tools you need to help you work effectively.

Chinese proverb: "There are many paths to the top of the mountain, but the view is always the same." May your path be easy and straight, and remember to enjoy the view.

· A NOTE ON THE TYPE ·

The typeface used in this book is a version of Goudy (Old Style), originally designed by Frederick W. Goudy (1865–1947), perhaps the best known and certainly one of the most prolific of American type designers, who created over a hundred typefaces—the actual number is unknown because a 1939 fire destroyed many of his drawings and "matrices" (molds from which type is cast). Initially a calligrapher, rather than a type cutter or printer, he represented a new breed of designer made possible by late-nineteenth-century technological advance; later on, in order to maintain artistic control, he supervised the production of matrices himself. He was also a tireless promoter of wider awareness of type, with the paradoxical result that the distinctive style of his influential output tends to be associated with his period and, though still a model of taste, can now seem somewhat dated.